FAITHFUL FOLLOWERS

RECEIVE
PEACE, PROTECTION AND PROVISION

LOUISE L. LOONEY

Faithful Followers Received Peace, Protection and Provision
Copyright © 2025 Louise L. Looney

All rights reserved. No part of this publication may be reproduced, stored in a retrieval system, or transmitted in any form or by any means—electronic, mechanical, photocopy, recording, or any other—except for brief quotations in printed reviews, without the prior written permission of the author.

Edited by Marlene Bagnull
Formatted by Crystal L. Barnes of Better Way Publishing LLC,
    crystal-barnes.com
Cover: Fiver.com rebecacovers

Scriptures marked MSG are taken from THE MESSAGE TRANSLATION: THE BIBLE IN CONTEMPORARY ENGLISH. Copyright C 1993, 1994, 1995, 1996, 2000, 2001, 2002, Used by permission of Tyndale House Publishers, Inc. Copyright 2017

Scripture quotations taken from the NEW AMERICAN STANDARD BIBLE (NASB), Copyright 1960, 1962, 1963, 19658, 1971, 1972, 1973, 1977, 1995. 2020, by The Lockman Foundation. Used by permission. All rights reserved. www.lockman.org.

Scriptures marked NIV are Taken from the *Holy Bible*, NEW INTERNATIONAL VERSION, Copyright 1973, 1978, 1984, 2011 by Biblica, inc. *TM* Used by permission of Zondervan. All rights reserved, worldwide, www.zondervan.com

Scripture quotations marked NKJV are from the NEW KING JAMES VERSION G, Copyright 1982 by Thomas Nelson Used by permission. All rights reserved.

Scriptures marked NLT are taken from the HOLY BIBLE NEW LIVING TRANSLATION, Copyright, ©1996, 2004, 2007, 2013 by Tyndale House Foundation. Used by permission of Tyndale House Publishers, Inc., Carol Stream, Illinois 60188. All rights reserved. Used by permission.

Scriptures marked TLB are taken from THE LIVING BIBLE Copyright © 1997. Used by permission of Tyndale House Publishers, Inc. Carol Stream, Illinois 60188. All rights reserved. Used by permission.

NOTE: *Some names have been changed to protect the innocent.*

"Take your everyday, ordinary life—your sleeping, eating, going-to-work, and walking-around life and place it before God as an offering... You'll be changed from the inside out."
Romans 12:1-2 MSG

Will What People Don't Know Hurt Them?

Do not steal. Do not lie. Do not deceive one another.
Leviticus 19:11 NIV

Decades ago, most families lived on farms. They grew gardens, raised chickens, and milked cows. Many of them took milk, eggs, and other produce into town to sell to grocery stores.

One day Papa went to the store to buy groceries. A woman who lived on a nearby farm came in with a pound of butter. She asked the grocer, "Would you do me a favor?"

The merchant asked, "What do you want?"

The woman hesitated a moment before she answered. "Well, I was about to churn my butter and hadn't put the lid on the churn. A mouse fell in the cream and drowned. I got him out, but we went ahead and churned the butter. Can I trade my pound of butter for a different one? You know, what people don't know won't hurt them."

The grocer rubbed his chin for a moment and then replied, "Let me have it." He took her butter and went to the back room. Several minutes later he returned with a freshly wrapped pound of butter and handed it to the woman. "Glad to be of service," he said. "Enjoy your day." She thanked him and walked out the door to head home.

As soon as the woman was out of sight, the grocer turned to my daddy and chuckled. "I went in the back room and wrapped her pound of butter in fresh wax paper and brought the same butter back and gave it to her. She said what a person doesn't know won't hurt them. Hopefully that holds true for her. What goes around comes around."

THINK ABOUT IT

Have you ever done something manipulative or deceitful to get what you wanted? Did it backfire?

A Miracle Touch

People brought babies to Jesus, hoping he will touch them.
Luke 18:15 MSG

It had been five years since Todd's daughter gave birth to twins. The night after they were born, she called him, crying. "The pediatrician just told me both babies were dying. If you want to see them alive, you need to get to the hospital." Her dad grabbed his keys and rushed out the door.

Arriving at the hospital, he asked the pediatrician for permission to go in the nursery and touch the babies. The doctor granted his request. Todd reached in the incubators and patted the newborns as he talked and sang to them. When the infants' breathing became easier, he went home to rest.

A couple of hours later, a nurse called Todd. She said the babies were slipping away, and the doctor suggested she call to see if he wanted to come again. He did. He hurried back to do what he'd done before. The pediatrician found a recorder and asked the nurses to record his singing and talking. The infants perked up the second time.

After Todd left, the doctor had the nurses play the recording and take turns rubbing and patting the babies. The infants were revived and were released from the hospital a couple of weeks later.

The pediatrician called when the girls were five years old to ask Todd how they were doing. He told him they were in kindergarten and doing great. The doctor paused and then added, "The real reason I called was to let you know that every time we have an infant in crisis, I have the nurses play your recording and take turns rubbing and patting the babies. There's no telling how many children are alive today as the result of what you did.

THINK ABOUT IT

Do you know of a time when God healed a person who appeared to be dying? Has anyone's touch ever lifted your spirit?

I Was Not Planned

*And my God will supply all your needs according to
His riches in glory in Christ Jesus.
Philippians 4:19 NASB*

In the late 1920s, Papa tore down the old house where he, Momma, and my seven siblings lived. He and my brothers used many of the materials from the old house to build a new five-bedroom home. Then, the Great Depression hit with a vengeance, and surprise, surprise, they found I was on the way. They didn't do a happy dance.

It was almost too much. Daddy wondered how he was going to provide for his large family. He could scarcely support seven children, much less care for another one.

He checked with his insurance company and found his life insurance policy would pay his family $3,000 upon his death. That would help clothe and feed his family.

Step by step, he climbed to the top of the windmill ready to leap. But he realized this would be foolish and was not God's will. It would be more difficult if his family didn't have a husband or father. He wouldn't jump. He'd work hard to provide for his wife and eight children.

Sometime later, a rail defect caused a train wreck about a half a mile from where we lived. The train carried carloads of grain. Daddy got in touch with the railroad company and offered to clean up the spilled mess. They were pleased to have this option. Four of the older boys in the family and some hired hands rushed out to save the wheat. They worked from daylight until dark for a couple of weeks. They found a number of places where they could store the grain. Daddy sold the wheat to farmers and ranchers throughout the region. He made $3,000, the exact amount his family would have received if he'd taken his life. He thanked the Lord for caring for their needs and for convincing him to stick around to raise his family.

THINK ABOUT IT

Has the Lord ever taken care of your family's financial needs?

Ways to Get Warm

*Half of the wood he burns in the fire; over it he
prepares his meal… He also warms himself and says,
"Ah! I am warm; I see the fire."
Isaiah 44:16 NIV*

When I was a small child, we didn't have natural gas or electricity to heat our homes in winter. We had two stoves. One was an iron potbellied stove in the front bedroom and a cookstove in the kitchen.

One winter morning my friend, Jimmy, who lived about half a mile from us, came to play. We were both five years old. It was too cold to play outside, where we could run, climb trees, and build roads to play with my brother's cars.

There wasn't much to do inside other than draw pictures and color them. I pulled out the cigar box of broken crayons my sibling had left from previous years in school.

It was Monday—washday. My brother, Bob, was outside helping Momma do the laundry. She had a large black washpot to heat water over a small fire and a gas-powered washing machine.

I started drawing a picture. Jimmy took one of the crayons and pushed it against the potbellied stove. I watched the crayon melt and run down the side. It looked like so much fun! We took color after color and pressed it against the hot stove. We didn't pay attention to the smoke it was creating. Some of the smoke leaked out the window. Bob saw it and rushed inside, thinking the house was on fire.

"Stop that!" he yelled.

Jimmy realized we were in trouble, so he tore out the door to run home. Momma came rushing in to see what was happening. The stove continued to warm the room, but she warmed my britches with several solid licks. I wouldn't do this again.

THINK ABOUT IT

Did you ever get in trouble for doing something that was fun, but was wrong?

What's the News?

They will have no fear of bad news;
their hearts are steadfast, trusting in the Lord.
Psalm 112:7 NIV

Growing up, we had an old ringer telephone that hung on the wall. We had what they called a party line. Three short rings let us know the phone call was for us. An operator at a switchboard in town placed all the calls. It was a well-known fact that she listened to everyone's conversations.

As teens, we made up stories so she would spread false rumors. It didn't take her long to catch on to our shenanigans, and she stopped paying attention to anything we said.

However, if anyone wanted to know what was going on in the community, they called the operator. If there was snow or ice, she could tell us if school was going to be dismissed.

One night around midnight, my dad heard the phone ring two short rings, which meant it was for a family on our party line. Suspecting a possible emergency, Papa got up and listened. It was the war department letting our neighbors know their son had died on the Bataan death march. Daddy and Momma would comfort the bereaving parents.

We lived less than a mile from the cemetery and could see it from our house. If we saw a grave being dug, my folks would call the operator to find out who died and when and where the funeral would be. The operator called people when she thought there was news they'd like to hear.

Think About It

In small towns, people stayed in touch with one another by
phone. Small groups offer comfort and encouragement.

Beauty For Ashes

To appoint unto them that mourn in Zion, to give unto them beauty for ashes, the oil of joy for mourning, the garment of praise for the spirit of heaviness.
Isaiah 61:3 KJV

It was in the wee hours of the morning when our phone rang. Our telephone operator was calling to tell us the house next to the church building was burning. She said people were afraid the church would catch fire since the wind was blowing that direction. The little town where we lived didn't have a volunteer fire department.

We jumped out of bed, dressed and hurried into town. People were spraying water on the side of the building, but the flames leapt across and caught the wooden shingles on fire.

Daddy, my brothers and neighbors rushed in to get everything out that wasn't nailed down. My brother, Scott, ripped off the painting our brother, Sam, had painted that was behind the baptistry.

We grieved as we watched the building go up in smoke.

Thankfully, World War II had just ended, and they were dismantling Camp Bowie by selling the houses and buildings that were there. Our congregation bought the church and moved it where our old building had been. It was larger and better than the little church that burned. Hopefully, more people would attend, and the church would grow larger and stronger than it had ever been.

Think About It

Have you ever known of a time when God brought beauty for ashes?

No Fear of Danger

Though an army besiege me, my heart will not fear; though war break out against me, even then I will be confident.
Psalm 27:3 NIV

Papa didn't appear to be afraid of anyone or anything. He taught his kids and grandkids to tackle every challenge with boldness and courage. He seemed to think nothing bad would ever happen to any of his loved ones, regardless of their age.

One day I went with my daddy in his pickup to the pasture to drive the sheep to the barn to put them in the pen for the sheep shearers.

Going through the pasture, Papa drove over bushes and small trees like he was driving a bulldozer. We left the pickup in the pasture, rounded up the sheep and herded them into the pen by the barn. Daddy fastened the gate and said, "Louise, go get the pickup and drive it back to the house."

My mouth dropped open, and my chin almost hit the ground. "Daddy, I've never driven before. I'm only ten years old!"

"Well, it's time you learned. I'll show you how." The car had a stick shift, so he took a small branch and drew an "H" on the ground. He followed it with the stick and explained. "The bottom left side is first gear where you start. The middle is neutral, the upper right side is second gear, and the bottom right side is third gear. You'll need to push in the clutch each time you shift gears. You'll probably not need reverse, but it is the upper left side." To make sure I understood, he followed the "H" the second time. "You'll start in first gear, gain a little speed, shift to neutral, and then into second. You'll go a little faster and end up in third gear."

I was scared spitless when he sent me on my way. I was so short I had to sit on the edge of the seat to reach the peddles on the floor. To see my way ahead, I had to peek through the middle of the steering wheel.

What if I ran into a fence or drove off the cattle guard and turned the pickup over? I didn't, but Daddy didn't tell me I had to push in the clutch when I needed to stop. I stepped on the brake several times when I got to the barn. The car hopped along until the engine finally died.

After that, Papa considered me to be an experienced driver and sent me anywhere he needed me to go to fetch things or drive into town to get supplies.

THINK ABOUT IT

What have you had to do that was scarry?
Did you overcome your fear?

Meager Funds

Then God said, "I give you every seed-bearing plant on the face of the whole earth and every tree that has fruit with seed in it. They will be yours for food."
Genesis 1:29 NIV

We never went hungry growing up, although some meals were not too appetizing. That included times we ate cornmeal mush or just corn bread and what we called "sweet milk."

Papa worked for my two brothers in their farm implement business in the 1970s long enough to earn Social Security when he retired. He received a meager $250 a month. Even in those days, that was minimal. However, Momma and Poppa not only lived on that amount, they saved a bit of money each month.

Food was never wasted. Momma kept leftovers in baby food jars. She would let Daddy pick the ones he wanted to eat, and she would eat whatever was left. The jars were put in a pot with a little water and heated on the stove. They never hesitated to share food with beggars or anyone who needed something to eat.

I'm thankful we have Jesus as the Bread of Life—fresh every morning. We can taste and see that God is good.

Think About It

Have you ever had to live on a limited budget?
Have you ever gone hungry?

An Angel Appears as a Soldier

For he orders his angels to protect you wherever you go.
Psalm 91:11 TLB

General George S. Patton led troops in World War II. He was nicknamed "blood and guts" because he was blunt and aggressive. The Nazis feared him more than any other general.

My brother, Captain Bob Lanford, was an officer serving under General Patton in Germany before the Normandy Invasion. One day, he and some soldiers were driving about in a jeep, checking the territory around camp. A soldier stepped in front of them and held up his hand for them to stop. The soldier pointed to a barn not far ahead. "Don't go any farther. That barn is filled with German soldiers and ammunition. If you get much closer, they'll shoot and kill you."

Bob told his driver to turn around and head back to the base. He looked back to thank the soldier for warning them, and there was no one there. Bob is convinced an angel kept him and the others in the jeep from being shot.

When they got back to the army camp, Bob told the commanding officer what happened. He sent a bomber to blow up the barn. When the bomb struck the building, there was a huge explosion. Indeed, it was filled with a large amount of ammunition.

The commanding officer thanked Bob for informing him, but Bob thanked God for sending an angel to protect his crew.

Think About It

Has there ever been a time when you believed an angel protected you?

Pure Water

And he pointed out to me a river of pure Water of Life, clear as crystal, flowing from the throne of God and the Lamb.
Revelation 22:1 TLB

In later years when Momma and Papa decided to move into town, my brother, Scott, bought the 180-acre homeplace for ranchland. Scott never thought the well water tasted very good, so after he purchased the farm, he sent a sample of the well water to have it tested. He was shocked when the report came back, "Not fit for human consumption."

Eight of us children drank that water from the time we were babies until we left home as adults. We were all exceptionally healthy. Perhaps drinking the contaminated water helped build up our immune systems.

My brother, Scott, sold the house in 1953 and it was moved to a town about twenty miles away. The people who bought it renovated it for their home. A family still lives in this old home that is almost one hundred years old. No one will ever drink the well water from the old home place again.

Think About It

Are you thankful you have safe water to drink?

WE NEED A DADDY

That is why a man leaves his father and mother and is united to his wife, and they become one flesh.
Genesis 2:24 NIV

There is a void in a home where there is no father for the children. Ruth's husband, Ralph, died of polio in the early 1950s. She was left to raise six-week-old Celia and eighteen-month-old Andrea. Even at that young age, Andrea was desperate for a daddy. She embarrassed her mom numerous times when they'd be out somewhere. When she saw a man, Andrea sometimes asked, "Are you married? We need a daddy."

Leaving church one Sunday, Andrea was four and Celia was two. Jim was standing outside with his parents who were visiting from Tennessee. Ruth started to walk past with her girls.

Jim stopped her and said, "Let me introduce you to my patents." After they talked a few minutes, Ruth and the girls went on to their car. Jim told his folks she was a widow. His mom whispered to his dad, "Jim will marry her."

Jim didn't hear his mom, but he did start dating Ruth. She would occasionally invite him over for supper. When he was getting ready to leave, Andrea would ask him to spend the night. He would say, "Oh, I didn't bring my pajamas." One evening after they'd eaten supper, Jim said, "I'm going to run back to my apartment and get my camera. Do you girls want to go with me?"

Andrea said, "Yes, and we'll be sure to get your pajamas."

Jim decided it was time to be more explicit and said, "Andrea, it's not right for a man to spend the night with a woman if they're not married."

"Don't pay any attention to that," Andrea remarked.

Jim laughed but said, "No, I won't do that."

After a little more than a year of dating, Jim proposed, and they began to plan their wedding. Ruth decided to invite her former in-laws. She knew it would be difficult because their son, Ralph, had been their only child. He was the father of the only grandchildren they would ever have.

Ralph's parents accepted the invitation to the wedding. Afterwards, Ruth's former father-in-law picked Celia up and walked to the reception table where Ruth and Jim were standing. He pointed to Jim and said, "Celia, who is this man?"

"That's Jim," she said.

Her grandfather replied, "No, Celia, that's your daddy now."

THINK ABOUT IT

How difficult do you think it was for Celia's grandfather to relinquish his son as the father of his grandchildren?

JUST A TASTE

*Taste and see that the Lord is good;
blessed is the one who takes refuge in him.
Psalm 34:8 NIV*

Taste buds aren't used when Scripture says, "Taste and see that the Lord is good." Our hunger for righteousness is satisfied when we feast on His Word. It is tasty, satisfying, and spiritually nourishing.

My daddy tasted things that weren't considered to be edible like cow feed. However, he loved good food. It was sad when an anhydrous ammonia coupling blew up in his face, blinding him in one eye and destroying his taste buds. He lost much of his appetite and was unable to enjoy food as he once did.

Momma didn't eat much. She was only five feet tall and weighed less than ninety pounds. She always picked the smallest piece of chicken to eat. When we encouraged her to take a larger piece, she insisted she liked the wing, neck, or back. We were convinced she chose those because she wanted her family to have the larger pieces.

We often invited friends, relatives, and church people to eat with us. One of dad's hired hands ate with us on a regular basis. He had Parkinson's disease, and his hands shook constantly. He used his knife rather than a fork to shovel in his food. My brother, Sam, and I giggled as we watched peas roll off his knife when he attempted to lift them to his mouth. Sam would try to think of something funny to say, so it wouldn't be obvious we were laughing at the hired hand.

My folks lived on a limited budget. As a cheap meal, Momma made soup on a regular basis. We called it refrigerator soup, because it was made from leftovers in the refrigerator. We only had desserts on Sunday. Sweets were a special treat.

How thankful, God's Word contains sweet messages for His children.

THINK ABOUT IT

Are you feasting on God's Word?

I Came Up Short

*Command them to do good, to be rich in good deeds,
and to be generous and willing to share.
1 Timothy 6:18 NIV*

I grew up, graduated from high school, and decided to go to Abilene Christian College. Papa drove me there to begin my freshman year. As he carried my baggage to my room, he challenged me. "There's a job out there, find it."

My folks agreed to pay for my tuition, books, and room, but I needed to pay for everything else. I was blessed to find a job working halftime for State Farm Insurance. Back in those days, I was paid fifty cents an hour and made a whopping $10.00 a week.

One day Eddie Grindley came to speak in chapel. He talked about starting a camp in New Jersey, fifty miles from New York City. He planned to name it Camp Shiloh. Children could leave the filth and poverty of their homes in the poorest section of New York City for two weeks. They would be able to enjoy a beautiful place in the country and learn about Jesus. Eddie said most of the children had never been outside the city limits. Many had never seen a cow.

Eddie was traveling around the country, raising money for the children to go to camp. He was also looking for volunteers to work, counsel, and teach at Shiloh the coming summer. I was so impressed, I plopped my entire week's salary in the collection plate to bless the children. Suddenly, it dawned on me that I only had enough money for bus fare to go to and from work that day. I was tempted to run after the collection plate and get my money back. But I was too embarrassed to do that.

I fretted all afternoon, wondering what I was going to do. I could go without food, but I needed money for bus fare to go back and forth to work. It was too far to walk.

When I got back to the campus after work that afternoon, I went by the post office to pick up my mail. I was surprised to see a letter from my daddy. I had only gotten one letter from him the three years I'd been in college.

I ripped the envelope open and was flabbergasted to see a check. There was a note telling me the check was from selling my bicycle and a little extra as a gift. The amount was exactly twice what I had given in chapel that morning.

THINK ABOUT IT

Have you ever thought you may have given more than you could afford?

Preparing for an Adventure

"Yes," Jesus replied, "And everyone who has done as you have, leaving home, wife, brothers, parents, or children for the sake of the Kingdom of God, will be repaid many times over now, as well as receiving eternal life in the world to come."
Luke 18:29-30 TLB

My roommate, Sally, and I definitely wanted to go as counselors to Camp Shiloh for the summer. However, we needed $100 for travel expenses. We started cutting corners every way we could. We had a toaster and a hot plate. We bought day old bread to make a piece of toast for breakfast. For supper we split a can of soup. The owner of the grocery store near the campus learned why we were trying to save money, so instead of throwing away fruit and vegetables that were getting old, he secretly saved them for us.

Two weeks before we were to leave for camp, I still didn't have enough money to go. The college semester had ended for summer break, and I was out of work. But there was a hailstorm. The insurance company asked me to work full-time for two weeks to help with claims. Indeed, God was my provider, and I was able to earn enough money to go to New Jersey for the summer.

Carey Looney, a graduate student, was organizing the trip. He had taken six others to work at Camp Hunt in upstate New York the previous year. He told Eddie he thought he could get twice that many for the coming summer. But as it ended up, sixty people volunteered to go. This would fully staff Camp Shiloh and Camp Hunt. Others would do mission work in New York City. It was abundantly more than Eddie could have ever asked or imagined.

Sally and I were so pleased to leave for an adventurous summer in New Jersey.

Think About It

Was there ever a time when your needs were met by the Lord?

CAMP SHILOH

Be strong and courageous, and do the work.
1 Chronicles 28:20 NLT

We could hardly believe our eyes when our Greyhound bus pulled in the driveway at Camp Shiloh. We were amazed to see a mansion with fifty-two rooms and seventeen baths. The sitting room had tapestry covered walls instead of wallpaper. There was a beautiful sunken garden in the yard with a statue and the remains of what had been a waterfall. It was located on thirty-five wooded acres with a small lake in the woods.

A friend of Eddie Grindley had persuaded a rich family to donate the inherited estate as a tax write-off. Eddie had made the decision to start a camp for poor children from New York City.

The place was somewhat run-down, so the two weeks before camp started, we cleaned, repaired, painted, and built a dining hall and kitchen in the basement where the campers and staff would eat. We also built cabin floors for tents where the campers and their counselors would stay.

One of the volunteers from a wealthy family had never done manual labor. When she was helping build cabin floors, she kept hitting her fingers with the hammer. She was crying. We suggested there were other jobs, but she determined this was a do-or-die situation. Ultimately, she held the nails between her toes.

THINK ABOUT IT

Have you ever been on a Christian outreach
in another state or country?

I Missed the Movie

*But seek first the kingdom of God and His righteousness,
and all these things shall be added to you.
Matthew 6:33 NKJV*

Carey, our assistant director, had been urging some of us to leave Camp Shiloh and go to Camp Hunt in upstate New York. My two friends, Sally and Marian and I discussed leaving. We knew we would have fun wherever we were. I told Carey we'd decided to go. Strangely, he said, "Are you sure you want to leave here? It's not nearly as nice as this. His response confused me, because he'd been begging for those who would be willing to leave.

The day before campers were to arrive, the staff decided to go to a movie in a nearby village. My two friends and I chose to stay at camp. We sat on the steps of the sunken garden to read the Bible and pray.

Carey had also decided not to go to the movie. He spotted us, came and sat down beside me, and laid his hand on top of mine. This surprised me. After we prayed and talked awhile, Carey picked up my Bible and started to walk away. I yelled, "Hey, Carey, you have my Bible."

He appeared a bit frustrated when he said, "Yes, I know. Come here, I want to talk to you."

I got up and went where Carey was waiting. He reached out and took my hand. "I have been watching you, and I really don't want you to leave and go to Camp Hunt. I'd like to get to know you better. Let your friends go and you stay here for two weeks. If you still want to leave, I'll take you to Camp Hunt to be with them."

I didn't know what to do. I told Sally and Marian what he'd said. They suggested I stay there. "After two weeks, if you don't think you're interested in him, you can join us."

That evening, I was in the kitchen washing dishes. The volunteer cook said, "You look disturbed. Do you want to talk?"

I did. I told her I had been hanging out with another guy in the group who was leaving for Camp Hunt, but Carey had asked me to stay there and get to know him better. I couldn't decide which guy I wanted to be with.

This wise woman told me Carey reminded her of her first husband who was a fireman. She said he was such fun and had a sense of humor like Carey. He lost his life in a fire. She remarried a guy a few years later who was very serious and somber. Her second husband reminded her of the other fellow I was interested in. She said life was so much easier with her first husband who was like Carey.

Her counsel greatly influenced my decision. I would stay at Shiloh.

THINK ABOUT IT

When have people helped you make a difficult decision?

Eddie Rounds Up Campers

Jesus said, "Let the little children come to me, and do not hinder them, for the kingdom of heaven belongs to such as these."
Matthew 19:14 NIV

Eddie drove up and down the streets of New York City in his old bus, honking his horn, and handing out brochures advertising the free camp for children. Kids ran after the bus as if he was the Pied Piper. They were thrilled about the possibility of getting out of the city and going to the country.

Carey went to farmer's market the afternoon before the camp started to pick up vegetables and fruit to feed the children and staff. He persuaded the farmers to either give their leftovers or sell them at a discount for the worthy cause.

The next day, soon after we nailed the last nail in the cabin floors and set up tents, the kids arrived on Eddie's bus. They were bursting with excitement. So were we.

These wide-eyed boys and girls were ten to sixteen years old. Most of them had never run through the woods or swam in a lake. Eddie had us check them as they got off the bus to make sure they didn't have head lice in their hair or switchblades in their pockets.

In my tent, I had a group of eight ten-year-old girls. One of my little ones had her T-shirt on wrong side out. I told her she needed to turn it over. "No, the other side is dirty," she said.

Think About It

Have you ever worked with very poor children?

CAREY'S PROPOSAL

But I want you to realize that the head of every man is Christ, and the head of the woman is man, and the head of Christ is God.
1 Corinthians 11:3 NIV

Carey and I started hanging out together. Our "dates" consisted of working side by side, eating together, and going together to farmers' market to pick up food to feed the crew.

This more serious relationship had only gone on for a couple of weeks before he told me to decide if I wanted to marry him, because at some point, he was going to pop the question.

The second round of campers left before the last weekend of July. Carey had arranged for the staff to go into New York City. He planned for the group to stay together as tourists for the weekend until Sunday night when the others would go to a Broadway musical. He planned for the two of us to go out to eat and to the top of the Empire State Building.

I was weak in the knees, because I thought this was probably when he was going to ask me to marry him. We'd only spent a month "dating." Besides, I didn't know how I was going to respond. After we'd eaten, we went to the Empire State Building and got on the elevator.

The building is constructed so you have to take two different elevators to reach the top. Just before boarding the second elevator, I turned to Carey and complained, "I'm nauseated."

He asked the elevator operator, "Where's a restroom?"

She shook her head. "There's not one until you get to the top."

In desperation, he asked, "Where's a trash can?"

She pointed to one in the hallway. We rushed there, but it was a wire basket!

Carey gave his best psychological talk to keep me from throwing up. Thankfully, I held it down.

We boarded the second elevator and zipped to the top. The cool night air settled my stomach a bit as we looked over the twinkling lights of the massive city. Then, he held my hands and proposed. The impact hit me full force, and I blurted, "'Scuse me!" I ran to the restroom and tossed my cookies. When I came back a few minutes later, Carey said. "Well, that's one way to say, "You make me sick."

I rolled my eyes but didn't answer.

Later that evening, we went on the Staten Island Ferry. I decided Carey was the one I wanted to spend the rest of my life with. I told him, "Carey, I do love you and I want to be your wife." We kissed and he held me tight. He then chuckled. "I started to propose by saying, 'Would you like to be Looney the rest of your life?'"

THINK ABOUT IT

Has there been a time when it was difficult for you to make a decision?

BACK TO TEXAS

Be joyful. Grow to maturity. Encourage each other. Live in harmony and peace. Then the God of Love and peace will be with you.
2 Corinthians 13:11 NLT

Home again, home again, jiggety jog. Summer camp was over. We left campers who had placed their trust in Jesus. Hopefully they would remain faithful and share the good news with others. Those of us who had been volunteers for the summer would have boo coos of memories to treasure for the rest of our lives.

Carey's sister and brother-in-law had driven his car to camp. They went as missionaries to New York City. Carey rode the bus to camp with the rest of us, but he had his car to drive back at the end of the summer. He asked me and two others to ride with him. We drove from Camp Shiloh to Niagara Falls on our way home. Carey and I reversed the order by going to the Falls before our marriage rather than on our honeymoon.

Carey took the other two counselors to their destination before driving me to my parents' home. I arrived there with one solitary nickel in my pocket. Whew, I made it!

That evening after we got to my house, we were sitting on the porch. Carey took a deep breath and looked at Papa. "Louise and I have something we need to talk to you about."

My daddy had an inkling of what Carey was going to say and responded, "This is a bunch of hogwash. I'm going to bed!" But Papa didn't budge. Carey told him about our relationship. He asked Daddy for his permission to have my hand in marriage. He waited a bit before he answered. "Well, I've always hoped one of my daughters would marry a preacher, so I suppose I'm okay with your decision."

I'd explained to Carey that Daddy had told his girls if they married before they graduated from college, he would no longer help with their college expenses. Since we planned to marry in early spring, Carey told

Daddy he would finish paying for my spring and summer semesters.

Papa was adamant. "No, I paid for all the other children's college education, and I'll pay for hers." Carey had never been so pleased to lose an argument!

The two of us talked about our background and laughed when we realized that he was born in a town named Winters, Texas, and I was born in a village named Blanket, Texas. He told people he was cold all his life until he found a girl from Blanket. We spent the first night of our honeymoon in a town named Comfort, Texas.

THINK ABOUT IT

Have you ever been happy to lose an argument?

I Couldn't Cook

The Lord will give you meat to eat in the evening, and bread to satisfy you in the morning.
Exodus 16:8 NLT

When we married, Carey discovered I couldn't cook worth diddly squat. I could pop popcorn and scramble an egg, and that's about it. That's not much of a diet.

Carey had lived in an apartment with three other guys the year before we married. He had done most of the cooking. After we married, he followed me around the kitchen repeatedly saying, "That's not how you do that."

I got tired of him breathing down my collar and said, "If you don't get out of the kitchen and leave me alone, I'll never learn to cook." He reluctantly went into the other room.

I was pleased when he told me his mom didn't know how to cook when she and his dad married, but over the years, she became an excellent cook. She told Carey the first time she made biscuits, she threw them in the trash. She took the second batch outside and put them in the dog's bowl. She looked out the window later and the dog was burying the biscuits.

Frozen orange juice had just come on the market when we married. I decided to splurge and buy some for breakfast one morning. Carey took one sip, frowned, and said, "How did you make this?"

There he goes, questioning me again. "I followed the directions on the can!"

He got up from the table, got the empty can out of the trash, and said, "How much water did you add?"

"Exactly what it said. I added three one-third cans. Don't tell me I didn't know what I was doing!"

"Good grief, three one-third cans is one can. You added one can of water?"

Wonder of wonders, I did learn to cook and spent fifteen years at a retreat center where I cooked meals for the retreatants. They thought my cooking was smacking good and often came back for seconds.

THINK ABOUT IT

Has there been anything difficult for you to learn?

Moving to Indiana

Religion that God our Father accepts as pure and faultless is this: to look after orphans and widows in their distress and to keep oneself from being polluted by the world.
James 1:27 NIV

Carey and I married when I was a senior at Abilene Christian College and he was finishing a master's degree at Hardin-Simmons University. After we graduated, he was hired to build an orphanage in Indiana. He would also preach at a small church there. The church let us move in the apartment on the second story of the church building. Carey would earn $200 a month overseeing the building of the orphanage.

I got a job teaching typing at Valparaiso University and was also paid $200 a month. I looked young and the students kept asking me how old I was. I told them I was old enough to teach. I refused to tell them I was only twenty.

Since Carey was a preacher, a doctor in town didn't charge us. Dr. Vietski took care of all our medical expenses. I'd read Dr. Grantly Dick Reed's book, *Childbirth Without Fear* and let my doctor know I wanted to have my children natural childbirth. Although this was not a common practice, our doctor agreed to work with me.

Dr. Reed wrote that fear muscles work horizontally, and the delivery muscles work vertically. The more fear, the harder the delivery muscles had to work and greater the pain. Nurses in the labor room said they couldn't believe how little pain I seemed to be in. Dr. Vietski allowed Carey to come in the delivery room.

Church members brought us groceries and helped with our other financial needs.

THINK ABOUT IT

Have you ever been provided for when you were short of money?

Eddie's Last Trip But Not His Last Journey

We remember before our God and Father your work produced by faith, your labor prompted by love, and your endurance inspired by hope in our Lord Jesus Christ.
1 Thessalonians 1:3 NIV

Several years after Carey and I were married, we got a letter from Eddie Grindley. He was the director of Camp Shiloh when Carey and I worked there. Eddie was still raising money for poor children to go to camp and learn about Jesus.

He planned to come through Denver and wanted to know if he could spend the night with us. Yes! It would be delightful to see him again. He was so loved.

When Eddie arrived, we noticed the years deeply etched across his face. He was thin and walked slowly. His shoulders were slightly stooped. "I'm so tired," he said. "I'll be glad when the Lord calls me home and I can rest." Despite Eddie's weakened condition, he was still upbeat and cheerful. We stayed up late talking about old times at camp.

The next morning, Carey walked Eddie to his car as he was getting ready to leave. Carey was startled when he looked at his tires. "Eddie, your tires are threadbare. They'll never get you back to New Jersey."

Eddie smiled and spoke with confident trust. "Oh yes, God knows I don't have the money to buy new ones, and I need to get home. I'll be okay." (Carey was working on his doctorate, so we didn't have any extra money to help him.)

About a week later, we got a letter from Eddie. "I made it home. The Lord made sure of that. But the next morning, I went out to get in my car and two of the tires were flat." I imagined hearing Eddie's boisterous laughter as he wrote these lines.

A few months later, we got a letter from his wife, Stella. "Eddie passed away a few weeks after he got home from your house. God answered his prayer. I'm sure he is being rewarded for being a faithful servant. And he is getting the rest he so desired."

Think About It

Do you have faith that God will answer your prayers?

TREASURE HUNT

*Ask and it will be given to you; seek and you will find;
knock and the door will be opened to you.
Matthew 7:7 NIV*

Christmas was just around the corner. Carey and I were both working on post graduate degrees at the University of Wyoming. He was working on his doctorate, and I was getting my master's degree. We were scraping the bottom of the bucket for money to buy presents for our four children. We could only afford to buy three small gifts for each child.

Even wrapping paper cost too much. So, the kids and I got out watercolors, cut potatoes in shapes of stars and Christmas trees, and stamped designs on paper sacks. This would have to do for gift wrapping.

I decided opening their presents could be a fun game and make the experience last longer. I'd call it their Christmas treasure hunt. Rather than their gifts being under the tree, they would be hidden in different places. We lived next door to the church building, so I had more places where I could hide presents.

I wrote short poems telling them three places they'd have to go before they found a gift. One child at a time would search for a present. If the one looking for his gift couldn't understand the riddle, their siblings could help them find where to look next. Simple, silly poems such as the following were used:

> *There's a gift for you to find
> And here's a thought to keep in mind
> Look at a place you put your behind.
> You'll be nearer the gift I've designed.*

Obviously, the next clue would be on the top of the toilet. They had fun looking for their gifts. With three different spots, it made twelve different places they had to go before they found all their presents.

The children don't remember what they got that year, but they will never forget the fun game. This Christmas is remembered as their Christmas treasure hunt year.

THINK ABOUT IT

Have you ever used a creative way to enrich an experience?

An Indentured Servant

So I saw that there is nothing better for men than that they should be happy in their work, for that is what they are here for.
Ecclesiastes 3:22 TLB

Travis and his folks lived a few blocks from my parents. Daddy took Travis, his grandson, under his wing and had him go with him almost everywhere he went. He'd ask him to help with whatever he was working on. Travis chuckled when he grew up and said he considered himself to be his grandfather's indentured servant. He never volunteered to do the jobs and wasn't paid for what he did.

One day, Papa picked up ten-year-old Travis and told him they were going to Comanche to look at a tractor. He didn't tell him he had a job in mind for him.

Daddy looked at the tractor and negotiated with the owner until the man agreed on a price he could afford. The man lived approximately twenty-five miles from our house and where Travis lived.

When Daddy completed the deal, he turned to Travis and said, "I think you're old enough to drive a tractor." Travis caught his breath. He had never driven any vehicle. He couldn't believe his grandfather expected him to drive the tractor alongside the highway for twenty-five miles.

Daddy showed him the basic steps in navigating the tractor and drove slowly ahead of him until they reached the highway. He then sped away, leaving Travis chugging along behind.

When Papa arrived home, Travis's mom, my sister, asked him where Travis was. Daddy told her he was somewhere between Brownwood and Comanche. Sis almost screamed, "Don't tell me you left my ten-year-old to drive alongside the interstate for twenty-five miles on a tractor! Go get in the pickup. We're going after him and you're going to drive the tractor, and my son and I will come back in the pickup."

It was another time when Dad's wild plans hit the fan.

THINK ABOUT IT

Have you ever had to do something that was far beyond what you thought you were capable of doing?

The Welcome Mat Is Out

Do not forget to show hospitality to strangers, for by so doing some people have shown hospitality to angels without knowing it.
Hebrews 13:2 NIV

My husband, Carey, used no caution reaching out to strangers. He couldn't stand to think of anyone being homeless. He went to the local jail to witness to inmates. One prisoner was to be released that day and had no place to go. Carey told him he could live with us until he found a permanent place to live.

The man was pleasant and offered to help around the house, but three weeks after he moved in, he found the keys to our car and took off. The police tracked him down and we got our car back, but he was sent to prison. However, this didn't discourage Carey. He wouldn't close his open-door policy.

Next, Joanne, a ten-year-old neighborhood girl who came to Sunday school, asked if she could live with us. She came from a large family who lived nearby. Carey welcomed her and treated her as one of our own. Her parents seemed happy for her to move in with us. She was a part of our family for a year. When we decided to go to Japan as missionaries, Joanne's mother told her she could go with us, but we didn't think that would be wise. So, when we left for Texas to raise funds to go on our mission trip, Joanne moved back home.

When we were unable to get the support we needed, we decided to move to Denver for Carey to work on his doctorate at the University of Colorado in Boulder. He found a preaching job at a small church on the outskirts of Denver. While we were living there, someone told Carey about a woman who had been in the state mental hospital for years. She was ready to be released, but she had no place to live. Carey offered to let her live with us. She moved in and stayed until she found a job and saved enough money to rent an apartment.

THINK ABOUT IT

How are different ways you can show hospitality to others?

SAVED FROM DEATH

For it is by grace you have been saved, through faith—and this is not from yourselves, it is the gift of God—not by works, so that no one can boast.
Ephesians 2:8-9 NIV

Carey was not only preaching and going to school, he also volunteered to be the chaplain at the juvenile delinquent facility in Denver. On three occasions, he brought girls from juvenile court to live with us for their six months' probation.

Doris was the first. Her mother came by the house several weeks after she came to bring her a purse. She left after a few minutes. Doris threw the purse across the room and shouted, "It's not *stuff* I want. I just wish she would spend time with me and act like she loved me as her daughter!"

Doris was at school when it was announced over the speaker system that all the students were to go to the gym. They were all in the stands when the principal solemnly named four students who played hooky that day. He said they had been in a terrible car accident and all four of them had been killed. Doris had planned to go with the students, but she backed out the last minute. When she heard they were all dead, she fainted and fell on the benches. She was never tempted to skip school again.

THINK ABOUT IT

Do you know of anyone who narrowly escaped being killed? Did they believe the Lord saved them?

How Often Should You Bathe?

This water symbolizes baptism that now saves you also—not the removal of dirt from the body but the pledge of a clear conscience toward God. It saves you by the resurrection of Jesus Christ.
1 Peter 3:21 NIV

When Carey was the chaplain at the juvenile court in Denver, a member of our church called him and asked if he would go to court for the trial of his son, Steve. He and three other teens had been arrested for shoplifting. Carey agreed to go. At the end of the trial, the judge sentenced three of the teens to probation for six months in their own homes, but one of the girls, Sandy, was to be locked in their facility for her probation. The judge explained that the police were called to Sandy's home on a regular basis to break up fights. Multiple family members lived in the house, and they were all alcoholics.

Sandy cried when the judge pronounced her sentence. Carey's heart of compassion was touched, and he asked the judge if she could live with us for her six months' probation. The judge was pleased to have this option and granted his request.

Sandy moved in and took a bath that night. When Saturday rolled around, I told her she needed to take a bath that evening because we would be rushed Sunday morning getting ready for church.

"But I just took a bath Tuesday night," she said.

I told her I was aware of that, but it was time to take another.

She argued, "I only take a bath once a month, and I've had mine."

I was dumbfounded but decided to appeal to a higher authority. "Let's go ask Carey how often a person should bathe."

Carey was in the family room reading the paper. He didn't have a clue what was going on. I asked, "Carey, how often do you think a person needs to bathe?"

He lowered the paper and smiled. "Once a month, whether they need it or not."

Sandy smirked, "See, I told you."

"Carey," I shouted. "She's serious!"

It took some time for us to make it clear that he was joking and to explain why a person needs to take regular baths. Sandy might have considered monthly to be regular, but as long as she lived under our roof, once a month wouldn't cut it!

THINK ABOUT IT

Have you ever known anyone who didn't bathe on a regular basis?

ABANDONED CHILDREN

*"For a brief moment I abandoned you.
But with great compassion I will take you back."
Isaiah 54:7 TLB*

Sandy, who was on probation from juvenile court, had lived with us about two months when her mother called us. She told Carey her brother's wife had deserted their four children. They were ages five, three, one, and two weeks old. Their father had been taking care of them but he wasn't able to do that any longer. Sandy's mom asked Carey, "Will you go get them?"

Carey agreed and wrote down the address. Hanging up the phone, he told me what he'd agreed to do.

"Carey, we can't take them. Our house is small. We have our own two children, and I'm pregnant with our third. That would make six children under five years."

He snapped back, "Do you think I should have refused?"

"Oh, well. I guess you had no choice."

We left our little ones with Sandy and drove down muddy back roads to a small concrete block house. A thin, disheveled man came to the door and invited us in. His sister had called, so he was expecting us.

The place was filthy, and there was the smell of burned food. The man pointed to the stove. "That burnt oatmeal is all we've had to eat for the last three days."

Flies swarmed over the one-year-old sleeping on the bed. The daddy led us to a shower stall where the children's clothes were piled on the floor. He gave us paper sacks to put them in. He went next door to get the baby.

The three children were put in the back seat, and I held the baby. As we drove away, the two older ones pushed their little noses against the car window and waved goodbye to their daddy.

THINK ABOUT IT

Have you ever helped those who were extremely needy and poor?

NEW HOMES FOR THE ABANDONED

But you, God, see the trouble of the afflicted; you consider their grief and take it in hand. The victims commit themselves to you; you are the helper of the fatherless.
Psalm 10:14 NIV

We drove away with the four abandoned children. We stopped to get formula at the store and picked up used clothing from the church. We had diapers at home. When we got to our house, I refused to bring the children's filthy clothes inside until I washed them in hot water.

After arriving home, I started to change the baby's diaper. It had been so long since it had been changed, it was stuck to her bottom. It had to be soaked off. I bathed her and rubbed salve on her raw behind. She was so nearly starved, she could only drink a little more than an ounce of formula at a time.

Carey bathed the children and scrubbed them until they were squeaky clean, and their hair sparkled. After they were bathed, their hair combed, and they were dressed in clean clothes, they looked precious.

I started preparing supper. As I peeled the carrots, the five-year-old grabbed the peelings and stuffed them in her mouth. She also swiped the lid from the baby food jar across her tongue. When we sat down to eat, the children grabbed the food with their fingers. We'd work on manners later.

I had a bassinet and baby bed. Their infant could sleep in the bassinet and our little one in the baby bed. The other three children could sleep with our other child.

The next day, people at church volunteered to keep the three-year-old boy and the twelve-month-old girl. We would only have four little ones to take care of.

The children's parents relinquished all rights to the children. Carey's sister, Helen, adopted the baby and the three-year-old little boy. His sister had been married for sixteen years and longed for children. Her joy was over the top.

Helen caught a train from Fort Worth and came to Denver to pick up the children. When she got to our house, we kept the children in the back room and had Helen sit in a chair in the living room and close her eyes. We brought the baby to place her arms. The three-year-old stood by her side. Helen cried tears of sheer joy as she counted the infant's fingers and toes and hugged the little boy. She was so pleased to have children to raise.

Over the years, we took in from twenty-five to thirty people live with us.

THINK ABOUT IT

Can you imagine anyone abandoning their children?

MORE CRITTERS

Even the animals—the donkey and the ox—know their owner and appreciate his care for them.
Isaiah 1:3 TLB

Rick and Chip came charging in from outside. Rick was not quite six, and Chip was four. Chip was holding a puppy, and Rick held a fuzzy little kitten close to his heart. Chip stumbled over his words. "Look what we found by the pond!"

I didn't share their enthusiasm, but my lack of approval would fall on deaf ears if I tried to talk them out of keeping the little animals. Under my breath, I grumbled. "That's all we need, two more critters to add to the menagerie under foot around here." We already had a dog, a tiny alligator, and hamsters.

The boys got one bowl for water and another for food for the puppy and kitten. That's it, encourage them to be full-fledged residents. The boys assured me, "Don't worry, Mom. We'll take care of them." I could count on that to last about three days and then, it would be my responsibility to make sure they had food and water.

The boys fluffed up a blanket for their bed and put it beside the bowls in the carport where they could sleep. That night the little pets snuggled next to one another in their new home. Where you saw one, the other was trotting close by.

THINK ABOUT IT

Have you ever taken in a lost or stray animal to raise?

PUPPY LOVE

Your righteousness is like the highest mountains, your justice like the great deep. You Lord, preserve both people and animals.
Psalm 36:6 NIV

Our new little puppy and kitten stayed close to the house. The kids loved them, so I let the pets stick around.

Sunday morning, we were all in the car and ready to leave for church. I noticed Chip wasn't wearing a coat or sweater. It was chilly, so I sent him back in to get a jacket. While I waited for him, I backed the car out of the carport.

Chip came out screaming, "Mom, you ran over the kitten!" Tearfully, the children clapped their hands over their mouths as they stared at the lifeless bundle of fur.

I was mortified. "I am so sorry," I said, "but we don't have time to bury it now. You'll have to wait until we get back from church." A heavy cloud of sadness settled in the car as we drove away.

When we got home from church, I told the children to change their clothes and go bury the kitten while I finished fixing lunch. They went outside but came rushing back in a few minutes later. "Mom, the kitten is gone—and we can't find the puppy. Do you think the kitten wasn't dead and they took off because it wasn't safe here?"

"I don't think so, honey. Go look again."

They came back sometime later. "We called them and looked all over, but we can't find either of them. What could have happened?" I had no idea.

The following Saturday I attended a baby shower at a neighbor's house. During the afternoon, the neighbor told the group, "The strangest thing happened last week. We couldn't find our little dog, Toto. One of our little kittens that had been his sidekick was also missing. They were gone several days. Last Sunday, Toto came back home carrying the dead kitten in his mouth. He gently placed his little friend beside the momma cat and looked at us with a note of sadness in his eyes.

I bit my lip, anxious to tell the rest of the story. The women's mouths dropped open as I explained the bond I'd seen between the two pets when they were at our house. Now, with near human compassion, Toto had shown true puppy love by bringing his soulmate safely home.

THINK ABOUT IT

*Have you ever seen an animal show
compassion to another animal?*

Touch Carries Messages

*I want you woven into a tapestry of love, in touch
with everything there is to know of God.
Colossians 2:2 MSG*

Papa felt a firm handshake meant you could trust a person. He said the only time he appreciated a weak handshake was shortly after a chainsaw chopped off the pointer finger on his right hand.

Tender touch helps alleviate pain and makes a person feel more secure. My children wanted to be held when they got hurt. Bill Gaither wrote a comforting hymn called, *He Touched Me*.

When I'm depressed or anxious, it helps if someone puts their arm around my shoulder. When I'm afraid and no one is around, I may hold my own hands or hug myself. Flesh on flesh is comforting. Some who suffer from severe emotional conditions curl up in a fetal position.

Babies need to be held and cuddled to thrive. There have been reports of orphanages in Third World countries where babies were fed and their diapers changed, but they were not held, hugged, or rocked. It is believed that some of them died from what was called a "failure to thrive" syndrome.

Doctors tell us a tender touch can lower blood pressure and improve the immune system. They say it releases oxytocin, a hormone associated with feelings of love and trust. It definitely expresses intimacy.

Think About It

*Are you sensitive to ways you can comfort or encourage others
by touching them?*

Dad's Old Pickup and His Bad Driving

"Be strong and courageous. Do not be afraid; do not be discouraged, for the Lord your God will be with you wherever you go."
Joshua 1:9 NIV

Daddy's pickup had dents, skinned places, and rust. He knew the pickup needed painting, so he found a bucket of leftover house paint and slapped it on the old vehicle. It wasn't too attractive, but it covered some places that were rusted or where the paint had been scraped off.

He parked his old truck in the garage and was disgusted when he kept getting a flat on the front right tire. My brother, Scott, came from his place to change the tire for the third time and decided to check things out. He discovered the culprit. It was a nail sticking out of a board in the front of the garage. Daddy kept running into it when he parked his pickup there.

Papa insisted on continuing to drive, but he was a menace on the roads. Driving down a two-lane highway, he would wander into the opposite lane because he'd be looking at the cows or sheep in nearby fields. Drivers would lean on their horns when he was headed straight toward them. He would whip back and mumble, "I'm not going to run over you."

When Daddy grew old, he had to use two canes to get around because his knees were in such bad shape. At times he would use one cane to compress the accelerator and brake and the other cane to push in the clutch when it was time to change gears.

When my father died, he no longer needed a cane or his old pickup. He became strong in heaven and totally healed. He flies with wings rather than driving his old truck. And he no longer meanders into other people's space.

He now eats at the banquet table of God where there's no limit to the variety or quantity of food. And no doubt it's better than the best food he ever tasted on earth. There are more luxuries than he ever dreamed of, and pain is a thing of the past.

THINK ABOUT IT

Regardless of how much or how little we have here on earth, heaven will offer more than we ever thought possible.

Keeping a Good Attitude

*Now your attitudes and thoughts must all be
constantly changing for the better.*
Ephesians 4:23 TLB

After my daddy died, Momma said she needed to move to a retirement home. Her eyesight was poor, and she couldn't hear the phone ring. She was eighty-five years old and had fallen a couple of times. We knew she needed to be in a safer place.

My older sister, Sis, insisted Momma get rid of all her old clothes. She no longer needed to work cleaning the house or working in the yard. However, our mother looked for things she could do after she moved to what we called an old folk's home. She would go outside and pull weeds in the flower bed and offered to put the silverware and napkins on the tables in the dining room, but they wouldn't let her do that.

The room she moved in was very small, with only enough room for a single bed, two chairs, a stand for a TV, and a chest of drawers. We asked her if she would be okay there, and Momma said, "Yes, I made up my mind before I came that I'd be happy here."

One day when I was visiting her, the man in the room next to hers was yelling. I asked her if that didn't irritate her.

"No, not really," she said. "I'm sort of glad I don't hear well, so it doesn't bother me that much."

One morning after breakfast, Momma started having chest pains. She went to the front desk to tell them, and they called an ambulance. They also phoned Sis who rushed to the hospital. In the emergency room, Momma told Sis, "I sure hope I don't keep Scott and Dolores from going to Australia next week." (This was her son and daughter-in-law.) She didn't. She left to be with the Lord before noon that day, and her funeral was a few days before they were to leave on their vacation.

THINK ABOUT IT

Do you make a conscious effort to adapt to the changes that take place in life?

Anxiety—The Common Cold of the Personality

Do not be anxious about anything, but in every situation, by prayer and petition, with thanksgiving present your requests to God.
Philippians 4:6 NIV

When calamities broadside me, anxiety and worry rush in to claim squatter's rights. My creativity becomes lost in confusion, and my hopes and dreams get stuck in the past. I rehearse everything bad that could happen. My overconcern about tomorrow destroys any peace I previously had.

Carey used to tell me if I didn't have something to worry about, I'd find someone else who had worries and join them with their concerns.

Worry crowds out productive thinking and thoughts become scrambled. Joy left the country with no forwarding address. Time spent in worry can't be redeemed. Nothing I write is worth reading.

My worries are between yesterday's anxiety and tomorrow's fear. I tend to flit from one task to another and accomplish very little.

Jesus left us with a legacy of peace that cannot be earned or purchased. He didn't spend time worrying because he knew His heavenly Father was with Him. This special gift is ours when we take every thought captive, and we have the mind of Christ. The Lord is aware of everything. His grace and mercy bring insight into how He can turn challenges into opportunities when we trust Him more.

Think About It

Do you tend to worry more than you pray?
How does faith keep you from worrying?

Are You *Grateful* or Grumpy?

Do everything without grumbling or arguing.
Philippians 2:14 NIV

Many people are picky about what they eat. Some only eat meat and potatoes. My friend's husband won't eat leftovers. He told her she and the children could eat them. Some children are allowed to choose what they eat. My kids were never allowed to tell me what to cook for their meals.

There are also those who only want to wear name-brand clothing. My niece was sly. She would go to garage sales in expensive neighborhoods to find cheap brand-name clothing. She would buy them, take them home, clip out the tags, and sew them in her daughter's jeans and clothes so she could show her peers the popular brands she was wearing.

Far too many of us grumble about the weather, our jobs, or inflation. There are those who marry who think they can get a divorce if their spouse isn't everything they expected. (And whose is?) We live in a world of picky, picky, picky.

We attended a church where an old man who went there griped constantly. He complained about bellyaches, poor crops, and ungrateful children. He had an ongoing list of grievances. The pastor got tired of his negative talk.

One Sunday, the preacher challenged the old codger. "I'm going to keep asking how you feel until some day you tell me you feel fine."

The grumpy old man shook his head and said, "I never will." He had the same attitude as Earl Landgrebe who was attributed as saying, "Don't confuse me with the facts. I've got a closed mind."

THINK ABOUT IT

Are there things you constantly gripe and complain about?

Learn to Be Still

He says, "Be still, and know that I am God."
Psalm 46:10 NIV

Those of us with Type A personalities have a hard time being still. A boss of mine told me, "When you die and they put you in a coffin, they'll probably have to nail the lid shut to keep you from wiggling out."

Time management is important, and I get upset if I'm delayed. I set deadlines and make sure I meet them.

Those of us who are go-getters are competitive. As eager beavers, we're typically high achievers and perfectionists. And we're impatient with slow people. We feel guilty if we relax more than a few minutes.

This driving force was intensified because I was raised in a family and a church that were "works oriented." My parents considered someone to be lazy if they didn't work hard every working hour. They were expected to do as much as they could for as long as they could. Our motto might have been, "Don't stop 'til you drop "rather than, "Shop 'til you drop."

At my church, we were taught we had to do everything possible to make it into the outskirts of heaven. We needed to be involved in as many Christian activities as possible. We hoped when we died, God would reach over the edge of heaven and pull us over to walk through those pearly gates.

We have high expectations for ourselves and others. We feel we need to be on top of everything. I was reminded that both my sisters were valedictorians in high school. I was not. I felt guilty. I must not have studied enough.

THINK ABOUT IT

*Are you slow and deliberate,
or do you rush around in a hurry?*

FOREVER FRIENDS

*One who has unreliable friends soon comes to ruin,
but there is a friend who sticks closer than a brother.*
Proverbs 18:24 NIV

My sister-in-law, Nan, and I had a great relationship. We loved to share funny stories. We laughed and we prayed. We made trips together.

As Nan grew older, she became weak and had trouble getting around. But she maintained her sense of humor. We read a book that was written by teachers, *Funny Things Students Say*.

Even after my brother died, I continued to visit her. One day, I arrived at her house and knocked on the door. She yelled, "Come help me!"

She had fallen on the floor and couldn't get up. We both worked to get her to a chair. She pulled and I pushed and the two of us laughed as we got her upright in the chair. She said, "I don't know what I would have done if you hadn't come." Not long after this happened, she and her children decided it was time for her to move into a retirement facility.

I went to see her in her new place. I asked if the food there was good. She chuckled, "Most of it is, some of it isn't. However, when I cooked, most of it was good, but some of it wasn't."

As her immune system began to fail, she was moved to assisted living. Soon afterwards, she was placed in hospice. Her son, Mark, and his wife, Marianna, who were missionaries, came home for a visit. Mark had prayed he would be with his mom when she died.

Mark and Marianna's daughter, Laura, lived with my son, Paul, and his wife, Teri. She was working on her master's degree in counseling at Sam Houston State University. They lived less than ten minutes from my house. Laura was very close to her grandmother, Nan.

Mark called me one afternoon and said hospice told them Nan was dying. When it was time for Laura to be home from class, I called and asked if she wanted to go see her grandmother. She said, "Let's leave as soon as we can."

"I thought you'd want to go. I've already packed my bag. I'll be over soon, and we'll head out." We made the two-and-a-half-hour drive and got to the assisted living facility soon after dark. We assured Nan, we loved her and told her she had been a great blessing in our lives. We sang her favorite hymns.

Mark was holding her hand when she took her final breath. It was graduation time. Good-bye, Nan, see you soon.

THINK ABOUT IT

Rather than spending so much time grieving the loss of someone, try to spend more time remembering the blessed times you had with them.

TEARS

For his anger lasts only a moment, but his favor lasts a lifetime;
weeping may stay for the night, but rejoicing comes in the morning.
Psalm 30:5 NIV

I cry easily. I shed tears when I'm sad and when I'm extremely happy. I can get teary-eyed when I see something of extreme beauty.

There are two kinds of tears. There are those that come with pain and grief and tears that come with inexpressible joy. Strangely, the two tears contain different chemicals. Tears of grief typically accompany loss. Tears of great joy often come as the result of some great blessing. These are as dewdrops of hope that can come in the darkest hours. The chemicals in happy tears contain endorphins and other mood-elevating chemicals that aren't in sad tears.

Some little guys are told, "Big boys don't cry." Not true. Scripture speaks of two occasions when our Savior cried. Once was when he shed tears with Mary and Martha after their brother Lazarus' death. The other was when He grieved over the ungodliness of the Israelites in Jerusalem.

One Scripture puzzles me: "You have collected all my tears in your bottle. You have recorded each one in your book" (Psalm 56:8 NLT). Since there will be no tears in heaven, why would God keep them? Do you suppose an angel might stand outside the pearly gates holding our bottle of tears? Might he hand the bottle to us with the admonition, "These are the tears you shed as earthlings. You're to pour them out before you pass through the pearly gate. All tears are to be left behind."

Samuel T. Butcher built a lovely chapel in Carthage, Missouri. He was the artist who created figurines called "Precious Moments." In the chapel, he painted two cherubim standing on each side of the gateway into heaven. A weeping child stands before them. One cherubim is handing the child a tissue and the other is holding a sign that reads, "No tears in heaven." Behind them are dozens of little angels soaring throughout the heavens. Each one represents a child who has died and is flying about heaven in joyful glee.

THINK ABOUT IT

What will it be like to know that sadness will never be experienced in heaven?

Witnessing to the Unlikely

I persecuted the Christians, hounding them to death, binding and delivering both men and women to prison.
Acts 22:4 TLB

The apostle Paul did a complete turnaround when he stopped persecuting Christians. God got his attention by blinding him. He ultimately gave his life to Jesus as Lord. It was difficult for his disciples to believe he changed.

It was difficult for me to believe rock stars become Christians. But there have been at least ten who were converted to become people with great faith. One of the most powerful transformations was in the life of Bob Dylan.

A Strange Group to Witness to

One Sunday morning I stopped by McDonalds to get a cup of coffee before going to Bible class. Shortly after I sat down, a busload of women came in for coffee. It only took a few minutes to realize they were headed for a casino to gamble. They were laughing as they anticipated how much money they were going to win. The Lord nudged me to witness to these women and tell them the Christian life is no gamble. This felt strange because they seemed to be an unlikely group, but the thought kept circulating through my brain. Hesitant, but feeling it was the Lord's urging, I followed them out to the bus and climbed on board.

I took a deep breath and spoke loud and clear. "I want you to know it's no gamble to give your lives to Jesus Christ. It is a win-win situation to be blessed with salvation and have an eternal home in heaven."

I'm not sure what I said made any difference to one person but glaring eyes followed me as I got off the bus and headed for church.

THINK ABOUT IT

Have you ever been challenged to share the gospel with an unlikely person?

The Lost Diamond

"I will make your battlements of rubies, your gates of sparkling jewels, and all your walls of precious stones."
Isaiah 54:12 NIV

Rachel was married to a very wealthy man and lived in a gorgeous home. She had a safe where she kept drawers of diamonds, rubies, emeralds, and other jewels. When her husband died, she decided to downsize. She moved the furniture she wanted to keep to a smaller home. Rachel asked Carey and me if we would arrange for an estate sale and take the smaller items for a garage sale.

While we were following through with her wishes, Carey picked up a Parcheesi game and wondered if our children might like to have it. When he opened the box, he was speechless. There was a four-carat diamond ring on top of the game's pieces inside. He called me over to show me what he'd found. We couldn't believe how the ring got there.

"The game might have been sold at a garage sale for a dollar or so," Carey said. He put the ring in his pocket and brought it home. We found a beautiful ring box to put it in and went to see Rachel. Carey handed her the jewelry box. "Let me show you what I bought Louise for her birthday."

Rachel opened the box and screeched, "Where did you find this?"

"I'd like to know how it got inside a Parcheesi box," Carey answered.

Rachel explained that years before, she and her husband had been in bed one night when the burglar alarm went off. They called 911 and began to hide all the jewels that were lying out. She yanked off her diamond engagement ring and hid it, but a burglar didn't show up. The next morning, they searched and searched but never found the engagement ring. Her husband ultimately bought her another ring like the one they lost.

Rachel gave Carey a couple of hundred dollars as a reward for returning the ring. She would sell the one her husband bought later and keep the original ring Carey found.

THINK ABOUT IT

Would you have returned the ring if you had found it?

The Pearl of Great Price

Again, the kingdom of heaven is like a merchant looking for fine pearls. When he found one of great value, he went away and sold everything he had and bought it.
Matthew 13:45-46 NIV

In Christianity, pearls are symbolic of wisdom and God's Word. They represent purity, beauty, and innocence. I think of the parables of Jesus as a string of pearls. The wisdom for understanding these parables is ours for the asking. "If any of you lacks wisdom, you should ask God, who gives generously to all without finding fault, and it will be given to you" (James 1:5 NIV).

My husband and four children's IQs were all higher than mine. I was low man on the totem pole. In high school and college, I'd made average grades. Years later, I started praying for wisdom. I went back to college to get my master's degree and only made one "B" in graduate school. As a writer, I now pray for pearls of wisdom to write treasures my readers will cherish.

"Blessed are those who find wisdom, those who gain understanding" (Proverbs 3:13 NIV). Wisdom and insight leap off pages of the Bible as one seeks to be more like Jesus. The merchant who found the pearl of great price knew it was worth everything he had. Jesus, as our Pearl of great price, is worth everything we have.

Think About It

Do you pray for wisdom?

FROM POVERTY TO RICHES

You must distinguish between the unclean and the clean, between living creatures that may be eaten and those that may not be eaten.
Leviticus 11:47 NIV

Jess was one of eighteen children. They lived on a farm, and his father sold produce to local grocery stores. He wouldn't let the family eat anything he could sell. They ate possum, worm-eaten fruit, and food that was getting old.

When Jess was in high school, he made a vow that when he left home, he'd never again eat bad food.

After he graduated, he drove a bread delivery truck. After a few months, one of his coworkers went to work for his uncle. He came back to see Jess after about a year. He was driving a car and wearing alligator shoes. He asked Jess if he'd like to make an appointment to see if his uncle would hire him. Jess was excited about making good money. He went for an interview and was hired by his friend's uncle.

His boss was very fond of Jess, because he was personable, a hard worker, and dependable. After a few years, he offered to sell Jess the franchises for his chain of fast foods in Houston.

Jess told him there was no way he could pay for the franchises, so the uncle offered to owner-finance them. He told Jess he could pay back his loan with his profits. Jess took advantage of the opportunity and became a millionaire. His friend's uncle was Colonel Sanders, the owner of Kentucky Fried Chicken. Indeed, Jess would never again eat yucky food.

THINK ABOUT IT

Do you realize the truth of the saying, "It's not 'what you know, but who you know' that makes a difference"?

A Strange Way to Get Attention

"Where, O death, is your victory? Where, O death, is your sting?"
1 Corinthians 15:55-56 NIV

Jeff used a weird way to get to visit with those he loved. He put an obituary of his death in the local paper. He had his wife notify friends and relatives when and where his funeral would be.

His memorial would be at their church. Relatives and friends came from far and near on the day it was scheduled. His eulogy was read, and those in attendance were invited to share memories of Jeff. (Little did they know, he was in the foyer enjoying the good things they said about him.) They sang some of his favorite hymns, and at the end of the service, everyone was invited to attend a luncheon in the fellowship hall.

Most everyone stayed to eat. After the pastor offered thanks and before everyone began to eat, Jeff walked in the room. People screamed, "He's not dead. There he is!"

Jeff held up his hands to get everyone's attention. He explained, "I have so wanted to see all of you for years and decided to pretend I was dead, hoping you would come to my funeral. There will be no need for you to come when I die, because you have shown you care. Please don't hold this against me, as you have made my day by coming. This has given me one more chance to see you before I check out the last time."

Think About It

Have you ever used a manipulative way to accomplish something you wanted?

Prison Changes His Life

Consider it pure joy, my brothers and sisters, whenever you face trials of many kinds, because you know that the testing of your faith produces perseverance. Let perseverance finish its work so that you may be mature and complete, not lacking anything.
James 1:2-4 NIV

Sid was strong-willed and controlling. His wife, Ruth, worked to keep peace in the family by being patient and kind.

They went out to eat one day. Sid ordered a hamburger, and Ruth ordered a hot dog. He wolfed down his hamburger and then reached over and grabbed the remainder of his wife's hot dog and ate it. Ruth said nothing.

One day, he opened the refrigerator and yelled at Ruth that it needed to be cleaned out. He then threw each item on the kitchen floor. He left the refrigerator door open and hollered at his wife. "Get in here and clean up this mess!" Ruth meekly did what he demanded.

He Paid the Price

Sid attempted to borrow a large sum of money but failed to get the loan approved. In an effort to get the money he needed, he filled out new forms. He listed assets he didn't possess. He mailed the application in. However, his deception was discovered, and Sid was sentenced to federal prison for mail fraud. His business and all his possessions were confiscated. Even their home was repossessed. Ruth had to move from their house into a house that was little better than a shed.

While Sid was in prison, he turned his life over to the Lord and changed from an ungodly man to a humble and compassionate believer. When he was released from prison, he was a different person.

His wife said he was so changed it was worth every penny they lost. He no longer was rude and disrespectful.

A few years later when he died, his daughter-in-law spoke at his funeral. She laughed. She said when he went to prison, she hoped he'd be forced to remain in prison for the rest of his life because it would keep him out of her life. But after he changed, she loved the man he became.

THINK ABOUT IT

Have you ever known anyone who became a changed person after they became a Christian?

FORGIVENESS IS DIFFICULT

Bear with each other and forgive one another if any of you has a grievance against someone. Forgive as the Lord forgave you.
Colossians 3:13 NIV

I thought my friend and I had a wonderful relationship. She told me incredible things about her life and was pleased when I offered to write her biography. I tried to wiggle underneath her skin and wrote the book in first person.

An award-winning author told me we needed to have a contract. He sent one he thought was appropriate. However, my friend said she didn't like the wording and refused to sign it. Since I trusted her with my life, I decided we didn't need a contract.

I finished the book after a year and a half and sent it to her for her approval. She liked it, but since my computer sometimes forwarded the wrong material, she wanted to send the manuscript to the publisher from her computer. That was okay with me.

A Great Shock

When the book came out on Amazon, a friend called me and said her name was the only one on the cover. It didn't have my name. I was shocked from the top of my head to the tip of my chipped toenails. On the inside of the book, it had Copyright, with her name following. It also had Author, and her name. I learned she notified the publisher to send all royalties to her bank account. I wasn't even able to order author copies.

My grandson, an attorney, sent the lady an email telling her plagiarism was a violation of the US copyright law. The penalty could be imprisonment and/or up to $250,000 fine.

This "friend" responded by blaming me for trying to steal her book. I was tempted to write her a scathing email, but my son, a pastor, told me to back off. "God will take care of the situation if you say nothing. You need to be aware of the Scripture, 'Vengeance is mine.'"

It was hard to forgive her. But I knew if I didn't forgive her, God wouldn't forgive me of my sins. I decided to let the situation go. I asked the Lord to remove my negative feelings. Worry, frustration, and anger would no longer keep me awake at night. I was given a peace that surpassed all understanding. A huge load lifted from my shoulders.

THINK ABOUT IT

Can you trust God to take care of situations you can't change?

Choosing to Be Positive

You must have the same attitude that Christ Jesus had.
Philippians 2:5 NLT

My sister, Ruth, went through many hardships in her life, but she maintained a great attitude. Her husband died and left her with two little girls. One was eighteen months old, and the other was only six weeks old. At the funeral she told me she possibly loved her husband too much, but I was to remind her, she should never blame God for his death.

She was six years older and bought me gifts. Although her job didn't pay that well, she bought me a bicycle and other wonderful surprises.

Ruth lived a positive life. She prayed and held fast to her faith when her oldest daughter was kidnapped, stabbed, and raped. She trusted God would bring them through the trauma, and He did.

When she was in her nineties, she was in constant pain. But if you asked how she was feeling, she would say, "I am blessed."

When her overall health declined, she was moved to assisted living and placed in hospice.

One day an aide entered her room. Ruth was breathing in a manner called a death rattle. The woman sat beside her and held her hand. Within minutes, Ruth opened her eyes, winked at the lady, smiled, and took her last breath.

We have little choice as to what happens in life, but we can choose our attitude. We can either be cheerful and a delight for others to be around, or we can be grumpy, so no one wants to be anywhere near.

Think About It

Do you make a conscious effort to maintain a positive attitude and to be pleasant?

Do We Have Guardian Angels?

"Because he loves me," says the Lord, "I will rescue him; I will protect him, for he acknowledges my name."
Psalm 91:14 NIV

I was speeding down a two-lane highway, driving from Texas to our home in Colorado. As I topped a hill, I came upon a truck that was poking along. I couldn't slow down quickly enough to keep from hitting him, and I couldn't pass, because there was a car headed toward me on the left side of the highway. I was faced with the possibility of a rear-end crash or a horrible head-on collision. I swerved to the right into the ditch and passed on the right side of the truck. Thankfully, the ditch wasn't deep, and I made it around the truck without flipping the car.

Carey took a deep breath. "That was quick thinking. Thank You, Lord."

I wonder how many times the Lord has protected me and my family from being hurt or killed. There are probably many times when I've not been aware there was any danger.

Another Time of Protection

We had just sold our home. I was packing to leave and climbed up on a chair in the bathroom to get the towels off the top shelf of a cabinet. Suddenly, the chair began to topple over backwards, and I started falling. But then, amazingly, the chair stopped in midair, and I grabbed the doorknob on the cabinet. It kept me from crashing onto the floor. Most likely, I would have been killed if my head had hit the tile floor from that height.

Did an angel keep the chair from falling over? For some reason, the Lord didn't think it was time for me to check out.

Think About It
How many narrow escapes have you faced in life?

A Servant's Heart

"Here is my servant whom I have chosen, the one I love, in whom I delight; I will put my Spirit on him, and he will proclaim justice to the nations."
Matthew 12:18 NIV

God called Jesus His Servant. In the job market, being a servant is considered an insignificant occupation. If I went looking for a job, being a servant would probably be one of my last resorts. However, it is considered the highest honor to be a servant of God. "In speaking of the angels he says, 'He makes his angels spirits, and his servants flames of fire'" (Hebrews 1:7 NIV).

I'd prefer to be the one who orders others around rather than being ordered around as a servant. Perhaps I could refer to myself as the Lord's CEO—Christ's Exceptional Orderly.

Jesus acted as the lowest of servants by being obedient to God and submitting to being crucified on a cross—the most horrible death imaginable. He also set a great example of being a servant when he washed the feet of His disciples—especially the feet of Judas moments before he left to betray Him.

A College President as a Servant

One summer when Carey was in college, he went to Arkansas to sell Bibles. He was allowed to stay in a dormitory at Harding College. When he arrived, the college president greeted him and took him to the dorm room where he was to stay. Entering the room, Carey was surprised to see trash on the floor. The president excused himself and told Carey to wait there a few minutes. Carey assumed he had gone to find the janitor. But when the president returned a few minutes later, he had a broom and a dustpan. He started sweeping the floor. Carey insisted the president give him the broom, but he refused. "You are our guest, and there is no way I'll let our guest do the work."

THINK ABOUT IT

Do you have a servant's heart?

The Impact of Touch

He touched her, and instantly she could stand straight. How she praised and thanked God!
Luke 13:13 TLB

Touch sends various messages. When someone rubs my back, it gives me a warm feeling. A hug tells me a person cares. My husband, Carey, a psychologist, told people to hug widows. He said, "They don't get their daily quota."

Christians are told to show love to one another in a unique way. "Greet one another with a holy kiss" (Romans 16:16 NIV).

A pat on the head sends the message, "Atta boy, good job!" A tap on the shoulder urges someone to "Keep hanging in there. you can make it." Love is expressed by kissing someone on the cheek. Wiping a tear from someone's eye speaks loud and clear, "I'm so sorry. I'll do whatever I can." When a coach slaps the backside of a football player, he challenges him to "Go get 'em."

Carey often felt compassion for people when he was counseling them. He showed he cared by laying his hand on their arm. He could express his concern without it having any sexual implications.

Incidents can be touching. It touched my heart when I heard about two young sisters who drowned in a flood. When they were found, they were holding hands.

Think About It

How do you show your concern for others?

Be a Sweet Aroma to God

As far as God is concerned there is a sweet, wholesome fragrance in our lives. It is the fragrance of Christ within us, an aroma to both the saved and the unsaved all around us.
2 Corinthians 2:15 TLB

Sweet smells make us want to be near special aromas. My husband loved the smell of a certain cologne. He made sure I always had some to wear.

"Everywhere we go, people breathe in the exquisite fragrance. Because of Christ, we give off a sweet scent rising to God, which is recognized by those on the way of salvation" (2 Corinthians 2:16 MSG). It makes me wonder, can we sense when we are near other Christians?

Mary poured expensive perfume on Jesus' feet. No doubt, she wanted to give the highest honor to the lowest part of His body. It was as if she anointed His feet for burial.

As a special gift, my brother Rex bought our mom a bottle of Channel No 5 when he was in the navy in Italy. It was quite a contrast from the barnyard smells around their farm. He expressed his love for her in this special way.

I love to think of our prayers as a sweet smell of incense rising before the throne room of God. "The four living creatures and the twenty-four elders fell down before the Lamb. Each one had a harp and they were holding golden bowls full of incense, which are the prayers of God's people" (Revelation 5:8 NIV).

Think About It

*Smells have a very strong influence on how
we think and respond.*

The Need for Encouragement

May the God of steadfastness and encouragement grant you to
live in such harmony with one another.
Romans 15:5 RSV

"Words can be bullets or seeds. We can shoot people out of the saddle with cynical remarks, or we can plant seeds of encouragement for them to be everything God created them to be. Encouragement has the power to transform lives. "The tongue has the power of life and death" (Proverbs 18:21 NIV).

Jake, the son of a friend, did fairly well his first two years in school, but when he brought home his first report card in the third grade, he had failing grades in all but one subject. His parents disciplined him but saw no improvement.

Ultimately, Jake's father read Albert Einstein's definition of insanity: "Doing the same thing over and over again and expecting a different result." This came as a wake-up call. Jake's dad and mom decided it was time to try something different.

The next report card had three passing grades. His father praised him. "Good going, Jake, you're improving. Keep up the good work."

His mom and dad searched for anything good Jake did so that they could brag on him—in school or at home. When he brought home a failing paper they had to sign, his dad would look it over and find a good answer. He'd compliment him, telling him he really thought the question through. As the months passed, their son became more cheerful and his grades gradually improved.

The Turnaround

By midterm, Jake was excited to show his parents his report card. He had all passing grades. By the end of the year, he was beaming when he told them he was on the honor roll. The family celebrated. Their compliments and encouragement had paid off big time. Jeff had been motivated to make a complete turnaround in school and in his behavior.

Encouragement raises self-esteem. When a person feels competent, they are more likely to be successful.

THINK ABOUT IT

When you want someone to perform well, do you tend to criticize or encourage them?

TEACHING THE INMATES

Listen to the sighing of the prisoners. Demonstrate the greatness of your power by saving them.
Psalm 79:11 TLB

When I was teaching at Darington Prison, I had to leave the house at 5:15. So I showered at night and laid my clothes out for the following day. When I got up in the mornings, I put the coffee on while I got dressed. I made a piece of toast and hurried out the door with coffee and toast in hand.

It was a joy to work with students who had been incarcerated. They seemed to like me and thanked me for coming. My students functioned on a third-grade level or lower. They were pleased with themselves when they learned basic skills.

I had a study period following lunch, but if I wanted to skip that, the principal would let me leave. The extra time on Friday afternoon made my weekends seem longer.

We had at least one lockdown a month when the prisoners had to stay in their cells for a countdown. I had to be there, but without students, I could grade papers or prepare lessons. I never had to take work home.

Each student was given a battery of tests on various subjects and given materials on their level. They only competed against themselves. We were not to use a red pen or give grades. We circled mistakes on their papers. They had to redo those until they completed them correctly. It was a great way to teach.

They Seemed Surprised I Cared for Them

Occasionally, one of them would say, "You act like you like us."

I'd flash a big smile and respond, "I do. Some may think you aren't worth a plugged nickel, but I like you."

I'd ask if anyone else cared for them. Many told me they'd never had anyone who cared whether they lived or died. So sad. I wondered if that was why some of them were in prison.

They were allowed to read the Bible in their cells. Perhaps if the Bible was read in school, people wouldn't end up in prison.

THINK ABOUT IT

Can you imagine how you would be if you hadn't had anyone who cared for you?

Finding My Bodyguard

"For I was hungry and you gave me something to eat, I was thirsty and you gave me something to drink, ... I was in prison and you came to visit me."
Matthew 25:35-36 NIV

One day when I was teaching at Darington Prison, a large guy walked into my classroom. He had bulging biceps and triceps. I pointed to him, smiled, and said, "There's my bodyguard!"

A couple of weeks later, he thought another student was being disrespectful. He picked up a chair and threw it at him. "Hey, wait," I shouted. "That's not the way you're to defend me!" Evidently, he didn't consider his actions to be inappropriate.

Since I had the lowest grade-level students, sometimes people asked, "What do you teach?"

I'd shake my head and say, "Not much." Some of my students could barely read, and none of them knew their multiplication tables or could do long division.

Could I Have Been Held Captive?

There was always a remote possibility of a prison break. If that ever happened, I knew I could be held as a hostage. When I was hired to work there, I had to sign papers acknowledging there would be no negotiating if I was ever taken captive. I was blessed that never happened. I was never afraid. Some prisoners asked me, "Aren't you afraid to work here?"

I'd respond, "No, I'm probably as safe here as I would be on the streets of Houston."

They'd smile and say, "You're probably right."

It's possible some students may have turned on me if there had been a prison break, but in my heart of hearts, I believed there were those who would have fought for my life if I'd been taken captive.

THINK ABOUT IT

Have you ever worked in a dangerous place or with those who were not law-abiding? If so, how did you handle it?

LIFE SEEMED TO BE OF LITTLE VALUE

*This is what the Lord says: "See, I am setting before you
the way of life and the way of death."*
Jeremiah 21:8 NIV

The Darington Prison where I taught is maximum-security. The principal told me I could look my students' names up on the computer in his office and learn why they were serving time, but he said it would probably be best if I didn't know why they were there. I didn't check them out.

It was one of my favorite jobs. There were no PTA meetings, no discipline problems, and no extracurricular activities. I didn't mind that classes started at six am. I'm a morning person, and classes were over at noon.

If a student ever gave me any trouble, he would be kicked out of class and never permitted to return. He would be sent to his cell first and then to the fields, the laundry, or the kitchen to work.

I had one student who continued to grumble about everything I asked him to do. I went to the principal's office and told him I was about ready to boot the guy. The principal told me to warn him one time, and if he continued to gripe, he'd be sent to his cell.

When I walked out of the principal's office, a trustee who did odd jobs for the teachers followed me down the hall. "Who is it?" He asked.

"Why do you ask?"

He snapped his fingers. "I'll kill him tonight. No one will ever know who did it."

Gulp. "That's okay, I'll take care of him!"

One day I walked into the classroom, and three guys were at the back of the room talking. Two of them challenged the third. "I thought you said you were a Christian."

"I am a Christian."

"Then what are you doing in here?"

The third man shrugged his shoulders. "I just killed a guy."

THINK ABOUT IT

Have you ever been around anyone who considered life to be of little value?

Would I Have Enough to Live On?

And it is he who will supply all your needs from his riches in glory because of what Christ Jesus has done for us.
Philippians 4:19 TLB

About six months before Carey died, he told me, "The premiums on my life insurance policy keep going up. I think I'm going to drop the benefits to lower the premiums." I took a deep breath and tried not to appear alarmed. He had been battling cancer for almost five years, and his cancer was not in remission.

I quickly responded. "Carey, let's not do that until your health stabilizes a bit." I was grateful he listened. When he died, I received full coverage from his insurance policy.

His friend, who was his insurance agent, knew my financial condition and warned me, "Louise, if you're not careful, you'll be broke in five years."

Although I was still working, my salary wasn't that great. I was fifty-five years old. I was pleased Carey's insurance money was enough to pay off the townhome where we lived, but I knew I would have to depend on God to provide any extra I needed. I would be forced to live on much less than when Carey worked as a psychologist.

Think About It

Have you wondered if you will have enough to live on for the rest of your life?

THE VALUE OF WISE COUNSEL

Plans fail for lack of counsel, but with many advisers they succeed.
Proverbs 15:22 NIV

I made a wise decision when my husband, Carey, died. I asked the four elders at church if I could get their input when I needed to make a major decision. They all agreed to give me counsel any time I needed it.

Soon after Carey's death, I received a check for his life insurance policy. Justin, a deacon from church, called me a few days later and asked me to go to breakfast with him. I was a bit surprised but agreed to go. While we were drinking our coffee, waiting for our food, he told me why he wanted to meet with me. Justin said he'd had some large, unexpected expenses.

He hadn't been able to make his house payments, and the mortgage company was going to foreclose if he didn't come up with $11,000 immediately.

He told me he had money coming in at the end of the month, but the mortgage company refused to wait any longer. Justin asked me to loan him the money so he and his wife wouldn't lose their home. The deacon said he would pay me interest and get my money back in a few weeks. I told him about the agreement I'd made with the elders. I'd need to talk to them.

Would I Follow the Elders' Advice?

Three of the elders told me not to loan him the money. The fourth one said, "Only let him have the money if you'd be okay if he didn't pay you back."

You probably know my decision. I told Justin I was sorry, but I couldn't loan him the money.

I was thankful I'd made the decision to check with the elders. I found out a year later Justin went to casinos and lost his money gambling. That was the reason he'd gotten behind on his mortgage payments.

THINK ABOUT IT

Have you ever lost money because of a foolish decision?

A Hot Check

But that same servant, as he went out, came upon one of his fellow servants who owed him a hundred denarii; and seizing him by the throat he said, "Pay what you owe."
Matthew 18:28 RSV

When my husband, Carey, died, I was grateful he had a good life insurance policy. I took the proceeds and opened a savings account at the bank. Then, I bought a single premium life insurance policy for $60,000. The policy would earn 6% interest, and I could borrow from the policy any time I needed money and charged 6% interest. (At that time, interest rates were much higher.)

I then flew to Oregon to visit my daughter. Two days after I arrived there, I got a telephone call. I was surprised when I realized it was from the president of my bank. He said it had taken him a couple of days to locate where I was. He startled me by saying, "Do you realize you just wrote a hot check for $60,000?"

Gulp. "Oh, no! I must have written the check on my regular bank account rather than my savings account."

"That's what I figured," he chuckled. "But I decided to try to get in touch with you and straighten this out before I had you arrested and thrown in jail."

I was so glad the custom practiced years ago by Romans was not in force. In the olden days, it was permissible to choke a person who owed money. There was also the practice of auctioning a person off as a slave if they couldn't pay their debt. I was thankful I wasn't being choked or sold as a slave.

THINK ABOUT IT

Have you ever been overdrawn at the bank and had to pay for an overdraft?

God Takes Care of His Children

And we know that in all things God works for the good of those who love him, who have been called according to his purpose.
Romans 8:28 NIV

We bought a farm five years before Carey died. After his death, a large amount was still owed on the loan. Hoping to pay it off, I decided to list the farm for sale with a real estate agent. It was on the market for four years without a single offer.

One day a CEO invited me to go to lunch with her. She asked about my finances. I told her about my inability to sell the farm. I told her my son, Paul, a psychiatrist, wanted to turn the farm into a Christian retreat center, but neither of us had the needed funds to do that. She became excited. "I know someone who wants to start a Christian retreat."

Following through, she called her friend and found he and his roommate from college shared the same dream. The two decided to look the place over and talk to Paul. They came and checked it out. They loved the rolling terrain—half wooded and half cleared. It had a small lake and a stream running through the meadow. The acreage was surrounded on three sides by a national forest. The men were impressed with Paul's credentials and pleased that he wanted to direct the retreat center. They agreed to supply the money needed to get it started. They had found their match.

Although the property was no longer on the market, the realtor who originally had it listed called and told me he had a buyer who would pay the full asking price. I checked to make sure the men who said they'd get the retreat started were serious. They assured me they were. They were ready to move full speed ahead. I refused the offer from the realtor. He came back with, "The man is willing to pay $10,000 more than you asked." I was tempted to take him up on the deal but held steady.

We jump-started the retreat, and people began to come. Paul, as the director, asked me to manage the center. He named it Hidden Manna.

THINK ABOUT IT

Has God ever worked in a situation better than anything you could have imagined?

Feed the People

"How many loaves do you have?" Jesus asked.
"Seven," they replied, "and a few small fish."
Matthew 15:34 NIV

We served the meals at our retreat center in the dining room of the house where I lived. We made sure the meals were ready when we told the retreatants to come eat.

One weekend, we had a dozen women come from a church in Houston for a getaway. When the women arrived, they told me they would be leaving Monday morning.

I Lost My Peace

My niece and nephew, Mark and Marianna, were visiting me that weekend. They were missionaries from the Middle East. I was thrilled to hear their stories of the miraculous work the Lord was doing in that country and in surrounding countries. They told me about Muslims who were having dreams and visions of Jesus telling them He was the Way, the Truth, and the Life. One family all had the same dream one night. Jesus appeared and told them He was their Savior. They all made the decision to accept Jesus as Lord.

We took a break to have lunch on Monday. My niece, nephew, and I had just filled our plates and were about to sit down to eat when one of the retreatants came to the door. She told me they would be over in fifteen minutes for lunch. I had no idea they planned to eat before leaving. I was "all shook up."

I rushed back in the room and told my niece and nephew, "Don't take a bite! I need the food to feed the women who are here on a retreat!" We scraped our food back into the bowls and platters. I groaned, "Oh dear. I don't think there is enough food for them."

Thank God, He was Jehovah Jireh, our provider. He made sure the women who were at the retreat had plenty to eat, and enough to fill my relatives' tummies and mine. It wasn't a matter of multiplying loaves and fishes, but God stretched the food so there was plenty for the retreatants, for us, and leftovers. The ladies went on their way rejoicing.

Mark and Marianna still tease me about having to give up their lunch. Thank you, Almighty God.

THINK ABOUT IT

Has there ever been a time when you didn't think you had enough food, and it appeared the Lord multiplied it so there was plenty?

What Do We Need to Leave Behind?

Why not just accept mistreatment and leave it at that?
1 Corinthians 6:7 TLB

Allen sat on the deck at Hidden Manna with the staff for our morning devotional. He talked about people who had taken advantage of him when he was growing up and misfortunes confronting him in business. He complained that life was not fair. We agreed. "That's often true in a world that is steeped in sin and with people who don't hesitate to take advantage of others."

As Allen was sharing his grievances, I watched a leaf dangling over his head on a spider web. I got up and yanked it down. This was a distraction from our devotional, but the leaf bothered me.

After we finished our Bible study, Allen went back to the Casa where he was staying. He sat on the porch gazing into the distance. A gust of wind blew dead leaves across the yard. He thought of how lifeless these leaves were as they toppled over the ground. He also thought about the dead leaf I yanked down that hung over his head.

Could those dead leaves represent his past that needed to be blown away so fresh leaves could grow? He prayed he'd stop mulling over his past and focus on a more promising future. By God's grace, he would not be so pessimistic.

Think About It

Are there things from the past you need to stop grumbling about?

A Dog Teaches a Lesson

And we know that in all things God works for the good of those who love him, who have been called according to his purpose.
Romans 8:28 NIV

Diane came to Hidden Manna, because she wanted a stronger relationship with the Lord. She sat on the porch at the Casa, our little Spanish cottage in the woods.

Our dog, Sassy, came to the gate and barked. Then she came to the porch where Diane was, paused a few seconds, returned to the gate, and barked again.

"I think the dog wants me to follow her," Diane reasoned. She walked to the gate where the dog waited.

Sassy started trotting down the trail into the woods. Diane followed. Coming to a cross, the dog lay down beside it. Diane sat on the bench nearby. She looked at the weeds growing around the cross. A thought crossed her mind. That's my spiritual life—filled with weeds. I seldom think of the Lord, I don't pray often or read the Bible. This hit hard. Diane got on her hands and knees and began to pull weeds. Tears of regret fell to the ground. She confessed her negligence and repented. By God's grace, she would renew her relationship with the Lord. It was a new day. She finished pulling the weeds and made a new commitment. Peace reigned in her heart. Thank you, Sassy.

Think About It

Has the Lord ever reminded you to draw closer to Him?

God's Nudge

*And don't worry about food—what to eat and drink;
don't worry at all that God will provide it for you.*
Luke 12:29 TLB

One of the main jobs I had at Hidden Manna was cooking the meals for those who came. One employee baked the bread and another made the desserts.

I was always concerned, wondering if we'd prepared enough food, although there had never been a shortage. There were always leftovers! The first time we had a large amount of food left after lunch, my "depression day mentality" kicked in. I never wanted to throw food away. I thought of the Good Shepherd Mission in a nearby city. It was a place where the homeless slept and were fed. I called the manager and told him we had extra food and asked if they were allowed to eat leftovers. He quickly replied, "Yes, how soon can you get here? We don't have anything for supper.

It is amazing how God used us to take care of the needs of others. We're never to ignore a gentle nudge from the Holy Spirit. It may be to make a phone call or reach out to someone. We may need to send someone a note. We're to listen for the still, small voice of our heavenly Father. He is aware of any need we can take care of.

We may never realize why the Lord prompts us to do something, but we need to be obedient. We are to continue to pray, "Speak, Lord, your servant listens."

When our retreat center was sold, we needed to get rid of the furniture in the three retreat houses and a mobile home. We called the mission and offered most of the furniture and miscellaneous items for them to sell in their resale shop. They brought a large truck and trailer to haul things away. It was an answer to our prayers and theirs. I had tears of gratitude when I saw the truck and trailer drive out the gate with the things.

THINK ABOUT IT

Do you ever do something you are nudged to do, even if it doesn't seem to make sense?

Nothing Is Impossible for God

Jesus looked at them and said, "With man this is impossible, but not with God; all things are possible with God."
Mark 10:27 NIV

Jon Paul was slow learning to talk. When he was old enough to go to school, he couldn't remember the alphabet and couldn't tell time. He appeared to be a slow learner.

One afternoon he listened to a program on the radio about a small boy who said words seemed to jump off the page and become scrambled. The director of the program explained the boy was dyslectic. Jon Paul told his parents he had the same problem. They decided to have him tested by a diagnostician at a nearby school. After the test, the diagnostician shook her head. "He's the most learning-disabled child I've ever tested."

Although this was discouraging to hear, his parents were relieved to find the source of his problem. They would home-school Jon Paul and do everything they could to help him overcome his disability.

As a diagnostician, I was afraid Jon Paul could never make it in college. I didn't check his progress over the years. I hoped he'd be able to find a decent job after he graduated from high school. However, he enrolled in college and didn't flunk out. I attended his graduation four years later, happy to learn he'd earned a bachelor's degree. I gasped in disbelief when they called his name, announcing he'd graduated Summa Cum Laude. He had made straight A's for four years.

I was even more surprised recently when he was offered a scholarship at three different universities. He accepted a full law scholarship at SMU. It didn't seem possible this was the same child who initially had such a learning disability. As a godly young man, the Lord appeared to delight in transforming Jon Paul into a brilliant adult.

Whether it is emotional, physical, or intellectual, there is nothing impossible with God.

Think About It

What a mighty God we serve. Prayer and trust in God can accomplish more than we can ask or think.

DEAL WITH THE PAST

But one thing I do: Forgetting what is behind and straining toward what is ahead, I press on toward the goal to win the prize for which God has called me heavenward in Christ Jesus.
Philippians 3:13-14 NIV

There are things I did in the past I'd like to forget, redo, or undo. I wish I could untie the knots and tangles that keep me tied to yesteryears. It irritates me when I allow those things I've done wrong to recycle in my mind. I keep remembering how I cheated on an exam in college and lies I told as a child to keep from getting into trouble. I've confessed and repented, but those memories continue to bug me.

Forgiveness Should Leave Memories Behind

One of Satan's conniving schemes is to crawl in bed with me at night, snuggle up close, and whisper how ungodly I've been in the past. This keeps me awake, and I twist and turn in frustration. Get out of here, you evil tormentor.

One of the greatest gifts of grace was when Jesus made a way for us to be forgiven of all our sins. There's a way to get rid of that dirt on our robe of righteousness. Confession and repentance remove all stains.

I read about the apostle Paul and marvel at the wonderful example he set by choosing to forget the years when he persecuted Christians. Although he killed husbands and fathers, rather than struggling with shame and guilt, he invested his time and energy by spreading the gospel and converting Jews and Gentiles to the Lord.

I need to renew my mind by praising God for forgiveness and remembering that Christ took the punishment I deserved. I plan to spend whatever time is left in sharing God's goodness with others and praising the One who has blessed me so incredibly.

THINK ABOUT IT

Do you spend more time being grateful for your blessings, or kicking yourself for all the things you've done wrong?

OPEN DOORS TO CHINA

Son of man… "Aha! The gate to the nations is broken, and its doors have swung open to me…"
Ezekiel 26:2 NIV

It was Christmastime when my niece, Claire, came for a visit. We walked down a country road where the trees stretched their limbs overhead as a beautiful covering. I told her, "I'd like to go on a mission trip next summer."

Claire responded immediately. "Let's go to China. I've taught six children in kindergarten that were adopted from an orphanage in Beijing. I'd love to check out their roots. Our principal where I teach is going there next summer. He usually allows three or four others to go with him on his missions." I encouraged her to check and see if we could go with him to China.

I told Jerry, a Hidden Manna board member, what we were planning. He responded, "My wife and I want to go with you."

I asked Claire to see if they could be a part of our small group. She called me a few days later to tell me we were all set to go.

As a doctor, Jerry offered frequent flyer miles for Claire and me to make the trip. Claire was overwhelmed. She had never even met Jerry and his wife, and yet they were willing to provide her airline ticket.

In early June, we made the twenty-one-hour flight. We checked into a hotel and went to the orphanage the next morning. We were thrilled when the little orphans sang "Jesus Loves Me" in English for us.

Since China only allowed a couple to have one child, many Chinese couples would give up a newborn if it was a girl or they already had one child. Not wanting to abort their baby, some women gave birth to an infant and then abandoned it. The police sometimes called the orphanage to tell them there was a newborn near a certain dumpster in the city. Someone from the orphanage would rescue the baby and bring the infant to raise with the other children.

The Christian lady who ran the orphanage tried to find Christian couples in the states who longed to adopt a baby. She wanted the little ones to be loved and brought up in a Christian home.

THINK ABOUT IT

Would you be here if your parents could have only had one child?

CHINESE CHRISTIANS STUDY THE BIBLE

I will study your commandments and reflect on your ways.
Psalm 119:15 NLT

Before we visited an underground Bible school in China, Claire and I were asked if we would like to teach a lesson there. We were honored to be given this opportunity.

The students came from all over China. There were twenty men and women in the class. They ranged in age from about nineteen to thirty. Some spend their life savings to come to study the Bible six hours a day, five days a week, for three months. After that, they return to their homes to teach, preach, or go as missionaries to spread the message of salvation. They consider it very important to know the Scriptures well. They plan to go to many countries as missionaries. Some plan to come to America.

They have devised a number of unique ways to be aware when authorities are headed for the classroom to arrest them. The students scatter so that no more than two of them will be together. They rush out in different directions.

The Christian students usually have to move several times during the three months, because they are afraid the police have located where they are. They are always on the alert. Prayer for protection is one of their top priorities.

THINK ABOUT IT

Aren't you thankful we can study the Bible and have church without being arrested?

NORTH KOREA

*He said to them, "Go into all the world and preach
the gospel to all creation."
Mark 16:15 NIV*

We'd heard no American could get into North Korea, but an optometrist in our little group had a suitcase of glasses he'd gotten from the Lion's club. He offered to check people's eyes there and fit them as best he could. Although the glasses weren't the exact prescription, the citizens could see better than they could without them.

When we arrived in North Korea and went through customs, they took our cameras, passports, and anything else they thought might be used in what they considered to be a devious way.

Someone asked me if I wasn't afraid to give up my passport. I told them if the authorities wanted to shoot us, it wouldn't matter if we didn't have passports. We wouldn't need a passport to get into heaven, and that would be our destination if we were killed.

We didn't dare take Bibles with us. And we were told not to pray or talk about anything spiritual in our hotel rooms, because every room was bugged.

Guards almost breathed down our necks the entire time we were in the country. The only exception was when we climbed to the top of a hill that was for sale for $1,000,000. Our guide said he hoped he could buy the hill and build a factory there to make bread for school children.

We Americans envisioned a time when it would be permissible to put a cross on top of buildings there and turn them into churches. We pray someday the North Koreans will worship our King of kings and Lord of lords.

The guide who built the other bread factories was able to buy the hill and would be able to feed even more school children.

Many of the men in North Korea join the army, because soldiers are given food. Thousands starve to death each year in that country. People are so hungry they sometimes chew on grass or leaves.

The government in North Korea is very opposed to Christianity. The year before we went, we were told a Bible dropped from under a man's T shirt. The police saw this happen and shot and killed him on the spot. Another man waved at Americans, and the police beat him unmercifully.

THINK ABOUT IT

How strong is your desire to teach the Word of God to those who don't know how to become a Christian?

I Was Almost Trapped

*I will exult you Lord, for you have rescued me. You have refused
to let my enemies triumph over me.
Psalm 30:1 NLT*

When we got ready to leave North Korea, we were given our passports and other items that were taken when we went through customs. My traveling companions were ahead of me. As the last one to get my things, I went downstairs where I faced two doors. I went through the wrong one. It closed behind me and locked! I realized I was in a holding room and couldn't get out.

The only thing in the room was a couch and a huge picture of Kim Jong-il with a fan blowing on it. I didn't see air conditioners or fans anywhere else in the country, but they made sure his portrait stayed cool.

When I didn't come out right away, the others in my group panicked. "They've got her. They've got her!" Thankfully, there was a high window I could reach by climbing on the back of the couch. I climbed there and started knocking on the window. My friends heard me and realized where I was. They rushed in to open the door for me to get out. Their panic turned to belly-shaking laughter over my foolish mistake.

Think About It

*Have you ever been trapped in a dangerous place or gotten
caught in a place where you couldn't get out?*

Ways to Spread the Message

He is the one we proclaim, admonishing and teaching everyone with all wisdom, so that we may present everyone fully mature in Christ.
Colossians 1:28 NIV

The man who got us into the country had attended a seminary before visiting North Korea. He was able to raise a large amount of money to take with him on his tour. He gave the money to a North Korean man he met who had worked in America and gone back and built a couple of bread factories to feed starving school children. The government forced this man to sign a written document promising he would never speak of Jesus, God, the Holy Spirit, or heaven.

Since he fed hundreds of children each day, when he turned sixty, they had a big celebration in his honor. He was given the opportunity to speak. Someone in the audience commented that he must have been paid a large salary when he worked in the United States for him to build the two factories. He replied, "No, a friend of mine gave me the money. He told me he had a Father who owns the cattle on a thousand hills." Many caught their breath, because they knew he was referring to Father God as being the source of the money for the factories.

There are millions of Christians in South Korea. At times when the wind is blowing north, they put Scriptures inside balloons, fill them with helium, and take them to a hill near the North Korean border to turn them loose. The balloons blow into North Korea where they fall. Citizens find them, learn about Jesus, and many become Christians. However, the one's who are converted must be very careful not to let the government know they believe in Jesus.

THINK ABOUT IT

How much faith do you think it takes for North Koreans to become Christians??

The Broken Teapot

As far as God is concerned there is a sweet, wholesome fragrance in our lives. It is the fragrance of Christ within us, an aroma to both the saved and the unsaved all around us.
2 Corinthians 2:15 TLB

Before we left China, Claire and I went to a tearoom where they served different kinds of tea. Our hostess explained each flavor had a different significance. The jasmine tea is always brewed in the same simple clay teapot. Each time it is served, the tea absorbs more flavor.

The night after we visited the tearoom, Claire had a dream that she was like that simple teapot. Each time she focused on the Lord, she absorbed more of Jesus' love.

The next day we went shopping to look for a little brown pot like the one we saw at the tearoom. She bought one at the market as a souvenir. She would put it on the top of the refrigerator to remind her to keep her mind on Jesus.

Claire was diagnosed with cancer soon after we returned from China. She died before the year ended. I was asked to speak at her funeral. I went by her house and picked up the teapot to explain how the dream explained she was saturated with the love of Jesus.

After we left the funeral, the little pot slipped from the bag and shattered on the ground. I was upset, but later, I saw a significance. Claire's life was shattered at an early age. But when she died, God's love was exposed. The love she had shown to hundreds of others would be remembered. The brokenness exposed the flavor inside. The fragrance that flowed from Claire would live long after she was gone.

Think About It

Are you absorbing more and more of the love of Jesus?

Teaching in the Underground Bible School

He shall teach my people the difference between what is holy and what is secular, what is right and what is wrong.
Ezekiel 44:23 TLB

A year after Claire and I visited China and she died, I started thinking about going back to teach in their underground Bible school. I would teach the Bible six hours a day for a week. I mentioned this to a friend of mine. She called me the next morning and said, "If you decide to go, my husband and I have enough frequent flyer mileage to take care of your airfare."

This seemed to be confirmation to move full speed ahead. I contacted the director of the school. He asked for a resume and three references. I sent them. A week later, I received an email. "You have been selected to participate in one of the most exciting Christian outreaches to spread the gospel."

A woman at church knew I was planning to go to China to teach and asked what it was going to cost. I informed her, my plane ticket was taken care of. She asked, "How much more do you need?" I told her they said I should have a minimum of $750. She pulled out her checkbook and wrote me a check for $1,000. "I don't want your mission to cost you a penny."

A Chinese church in Houston offered to translate all my notes into Chinese. That was about thirty-six single-spaced typed pages. The choir director at this Chinese church offered to make a CD of Mandarin contemporary songs to take. A group in The Woodlands had a CD with various translations of the Bible, a concordance, and many sermons in Chinese. They offered to sell these to me for $1.00 each. I bought 100 to give away.

A friend decided to go with me. She would go on tours while I taught. I made two copies of the Chinese notes and divided those and the CDs between the two of us. We planned to go through different custom lines at the Chinese airport. If one of us had our materials confiscated, hopefully the other could slip through. Thankfully, both of us got our materials safely into China. The director of the school told me he could have copies made of the notes to give to each of the students.

Two Christian taxi drivers rotated picking me up at the hotel and taking me to class. My interpreter, who was also my hostess, came with the taxi drivers. She had me lie down in the back seat of the taxi in certain areas, because she didn't want an official to see an American in the poor part of the city where the students met.

THINK ABOUT IT

What would you be willing to pay to study the Bible?

A Coworker Goes to Help Teach

And then he told them, "You are to go into all the world
And preach the Good News to everyone, everywhere."
Mark 16:15 TLB

The next year, I was rolling the idea around in my head about going back to teach in the underground Bible school. My niece, Lynn, sent me an email and asked, "Do you plan to go back to China this year?" I told her I wasn't sure, but I was thinking about it. She said, "If you decide to go, I will pay for the entire trip." This confirmed the fact I was to return. She sent me a check for $2,500.

A friend, Ann, who had worked with me at Hidden Manna, decided she wanted to go with me. We were both hams and decided to do skits to illustrate the lessons I taught. I planned to teach on the fruit of the Spirit as well as a few other topics.

The skits were well received, and the students said the skits gave them a better understanding of my lessons. One topic I taught was on forgiveness. I explained what a blessing it was for Father God to offer His Son on the cross for our sins to be forgiven. The students lay on their faces on the floor, confessing their sins. They asked for forgiveness and thanked Jesus for His willingness to die for them.

One of the girls in the class had been thrown in jail. The authorities arrested her in a worship service. I asked her if she would tell me about her experience. She bowed her head and shook it. "No," she said. Obviously, she didn't want to think about how she had been treated. It is amazing that after this experience, she dared to come to the Bible school and risk being sent to prison again.

The class members were the kind of students a teacher dreams of. They were constantly flipping through their Bibles, taking notes, and paying rapt attention. They were serious about changing the world by leading people to Jesus.

THINK ABOUT IT

All the students knew they risked being thrown in prison for studying the Bible. What would you be willing to risk?

The Third Trip to the Underground School

Do your best to present yourself to God as one approved, a worker who does not need to be ashamed and who correctly handles the word of truth.
2 Timothy 2:15 NIV

People heard I was going back to China to teach in the underground Bible school. They began coming up to me at church and handing me money. A woman I'd been friends with in a former church sent me a check for $1,000. When it was time to leave, all my expenses were covered. Thankfully, I could use the same material I'd prepared previously, because it would be a different group. Ann decided to go again.

Time passed quickly for us to be on our way. The third day after our arrival, when we were getting ready to leave the hotel to teach the class, the director called and told Ann and me to walk to a shopping center nearby to catch our taxi. There were policemen around the front of the hotel. She didn't want us to risk being followed. Every precaution was taken to keep police from finding the underground school. We followed her instructions and caught the taxi at the shopping center.

When we got to the classroom, we found they had no power. Since they didn't have electricity, the water pump didn't work, and they had no water. I had them call a taxi to take Ann, our interpreter, and me into town to buy water. Before we left, I asked the students if there was anything else they would like us to get. They were hesitant to suggest anything, but I insisted. One boy said, "It would be really nice to have a little meat."

Ann and I were delighted to buy water, meat, and fruit. They were so excited when we got back, they asked us to take a picture of them holding the fruit. We received a sweet thank you note from all the students.

The following Sunday, we went to an underground church. The worship was inspiring. It was obvious the Holy Spirit flowed as a fresh breath of air. We were hugged and treated as if we were long-lost sisters.

My interpreter came rushing in during the middle of the service and told Ann and me to get out. "Hurry down the stairs and out the back door. Authorities are coming in the front door downstairs." She told us there would be a taxi waiting to take us back to the hotel. As I was rushing out, I stumbled on the stairs and started to fall. Thankfully, I caught myself and didn't tumble down the stairs. We hopped in the taxi and escaped without being caught.

Had we been arrested, we probably wouldn't have been hauled off to jail, but we would have been deported and never allowed to come back to China.

THINK ABOUT IT

Has the Lord ever helped you get away from somewhere you needed to escape?

My Last Trip to China

*The glory of the young is their strength;
the gray hair of experience is the splendor of the old.
Proverbs 20:29 NLT*

I decided to teach in the underground Bible school in China one last time. I was seventy-six years old and thought this should probably wrap up my visits. Ann wanted to go again. We were blessed when the church I attended had a barbeque dinner and sold tickets. They raised enough money to cover both our expenses.

Unknown to Ann and me, there was a spy in the class. He had weaseled in to try to find out the addresses of all the students, so authorities could arrest them and their families. I thought this guy acted a bit strange, but I didn't dream he was a spy. The students realized there was a wolf among the sheep who had finagled his way into the class. One night at midnight, the students packed their things and sneaked out when he was asleep. They escaped Satan's scheme to have their families and them arrested.

Every day, after the taxi driver picked us up after class, he would stop on the way back to the hotel and get out and go to the back of the car before driving us to our destination. I asked my hostess what he was doing. She explained that he had numbers with the color and size of the ones on his license plate. He would tape this over his license. If officers became suspicious of him always carrying two American women around, they wouldn't be able to track him down, because of these fake license numbers.

A Going Away Gift

A Chinese friend we met offered to take us out to eat as a going away gift. She wanted to take us to a Korean restaurant. They had menus written in English. I was repulsed when I saw three things on the menu that were listed as "dog." One was "raw dog." Yuck! I wasn't too interested in eating anything there, but I tried not to show how sickened I was about the "dog" options on the menu.

A Chinese man offered to take us to get a massage. I thought they were going to pound us into mush. Neither of these gifts were as treasured as they were supposed to be!

THINK ABOUT IT

Have you ever been treated kindly by a citizen of a foreign country?

CHINESE CHRISTIANS

*Be very careful . . . to love the Lord your God, to walk in
obedience to him, to keep his commands, to hold fast to him and
to serve him with all your heart and with all your soul.*
Joshua 22:5 NIV

We met a Christian woman in an underground church who was born and raised in a Christian home in China. Her father had been beaten so severely for his faith, he could hardly walk. He limped and used a cane for the rest of his life, but he never lost his faith. Over the years, one woman's mother had hand copied the entire Bible.

When one young girl was twelve, authorities sent her to an institution for two years to brainwash her and destroy her faith. But she maintained a solid relationship with her heavenly Father.

One young lady was able to take piano lessons. She found a long piece of paper and drew a piano keyboard on it. She taught music lessons on that paper to earn a little grocery money. She found a woman who had a piano who allowed her students to come once a week to play it.

As a young person, a woman told us she was a part of the 1989 *Tiananmen* Square protest. where the police mowed down protestors with machine guns. She was wearing high- heeled shoes and when she turned to run, a heel on one shoe broke and she fell. When she did, the man immediately in front of her was shot and killed. The bullet would have taken her life if the heel on her shoe had not broken

The Chinese government claimed there were over 3,000 injured and more than 200 individuals killed that night. Western sources, however, were skeptical of the Chinese report and believe thousands were probably killed.

People from the states have learned innovative ways to sneak Bibles into the country and deliver them to Chinese Christians who cherish even bits and pieces of God's Word. They keep these hidden, so that they are not found in their homes.

One of the women we became friends with is probably the most incredible woman I've ever met. I asked her where she lived. She paused a bit and then said, "Oh, I sleep anywhere I find myself at night. Obviously, she has no home. Amazing. She always seemed to be neat and clean.

THINK ABOUT IT

How important is it for you to have a Bible to read?
Do you read it regularly?

CHRISTIANS SPEND TIME IN PRISON

But seek first his kingdom and his righteousness, and all these things will be given to you as well.
Matthew 6:33 NIV

One woman was caught reading the Bible in North Korea and thrown in a prison cell with about twenty other women. She led all of them to Christ. She said she thought one of the women had gray hair, but when she got close to her, she discovered the woman's hair was covered with lice and white nits.

Another woman who had been in prison said she was glad she didn't see very well, because she couldn't see the bugs floating in the thin soup she was served. The prisoners were only given enough food to keep them alive. One prison cell a prisoner was in was so small, she couldn't lie down. She had to either stand, squat, or sit. This woman has suffered in prison three times in China and once in North Korea.

One day this woman was told that she would be shot the following day. She asked if she could have one last request. They asked what she wanted, and she said, "I'd like to sing." They granted her appeal. She sang *Amazing Grace* and one other Christian hymn. As she looked through the bars, some of the guards had tears trickling down their cheeks. For some unknown reason, they didn't shoot her.

One Regret

After being released, one of the Christian prisoners told us the one thing she regretted about being in prison is that she had not memorized more Scripture so she could quote verses over and over while behind bars. Prayer helps keep some of them from sinking into the depth of depression in those horrible places. Most, if not all of them, have no regrets that they became a Christian.

As I mentioned, it is likely one of the Christian women we became friends with has no home. It made me somewhat uncomfortable, because she gave me gifts each time I came. She even gave me a strand of cultured pearls. I wondered if she even had enough to eat.

THINK ABOUT IT

Have you ever gone on a mission trip or helped support any missionaries who work in foreign countries?

(NOTE: IN SEVERAL OF THE STORIES ABOUT CHINA AND NORTH KOREA, THE SITUATIONS HAVE BEEN SLIGHTLY CHANGED SO THE CHRISTIANS OR THEIR TACTICS CAN'T BE IDENTIFIED. SOME INCIDENTS ARE ATTRIBUTED TO DIFFERENT ONES.)

Creativity in Quiet Times

*He makes me lie down in green pastures, he leads me beside
quiet waters, he refreshes my soul.
Psalm 23:2-3 NIV*

I started writing books after retiring from Hidden Manna. Creative ideas popped in my head when I was quiet and still. They came when I was about to fall asleep at night. I continue to think of interesting or great thoughts when I'm lying in bed at night. I'm sure I'll remember what I am thinking the next morning when I wake up. But if I don't get up, flip on the light, and write the idea down, it goes back to sleep and never wakes up. I now keep a flashlight, paper, and pen on the stand beside my bed to make sure I don't lose anything interesting or creative. Quiet times seem to be an atmosphere where great ideas are born.

The Reason for the Sabbath

The Lord had a reason for us to keep the Sabbath and not do anything on the sixth day. We need a day of rest and meditation. Sleep is also needed to be productive. Sleep removes toxins that build up when we're awake. Rest reduces stress, helps fight disease, and improves our immune system.

Think About It

*We need to use quiet times to relax and listen
for the still, small voice of God.*

Completing My Husband's Goal

He who began a good work in you will carry it on to completion until the day of Christ Jesus.
Philippians 1:6 NIV

My husband, Carey, a psychologist, was writing a book, but he died before he finished it. He wrote about ways people could fill their emotional "reservoirs" with Living Water. He wanted those who read his book to have overflowing cups that would spill into the lives of those surrounding them.

After he'd been gone a couple of decades, I decided to pull out his yellowed notes I'd tucked away. I wanted to publish the book in his honor. After several unsuccessful attempts to put flesh and muscle on the skeleton of his writing, I prayed for wisdom to breathe life into his dream. The Holy Spirit whispered, "Use your own voice to write the book, not his." When I did this, the writing came alive, and I was able to complete the book.

The various themes he wrote about sparkled with heartwarming stories and insight on how to live a Christlike life. He used humor to show how our own needs are met when we have joy in our hearts.

People could identify with the stories and illustrations Carey gave. The book would have universal appeal.

When I published the book, I asked the Lord to pull back the clouds and let Carey look down from the throne room to see how his dream had become a reality.

It is my prayer that his message will transform the lives of God's children so they will receive the legacy of peace and joy his book left for them. I named the book *Splashes of Living Water*. I hope it contains stepping stones leading to golden streets where Christians will hear our

Father's greeting, "Welcome home, faithful child."

THINK ABOUT IT

Have you ever helped someone fulfill their dream?

It's Hard to Slow Down

He says, "Be still, and know that I am God."
Psalm 46:10 NIV

A difficult Scripture to follow in modern times is "be still and know that I am God." We rush to get our food ready by using a microwave or grabbing a bite to eat at a fast-food drive through. We speed down the highway to get to our destination. We get irritated waiting for a light to change. If the person ahead doesn't move forward two seconds after the light turns green, we honk our horn.

In college, I ate hurriedly, because I only had fifteen minutes after class to grab a sandwich and catch the bus to go to work in the afternoon. After we married, my husband fussed at me, "You don't have to eat so fast. We aren't in a hurry to go anywhere."

I taught speed-reading in college, so reading is no longer leisurely and relaxing. This motivated me to hurry through life. I want instant gratification in whatever I'm doing. There was a time when people stopped to smell the roses, but now we only glimpse at them as we rush on by.

Time zips on, and days and years vanish in thin air. I'm not too excited about growing old, because it's forcing me to slow down to keep from falling on my face. I realize it is time to move out of the fast lane and allow others to pass on by.

Just as nature must adapt to the fall season of the year, it is essential for us to adapt to the fall season of life. The prime of life remains in the past.

I can identify with an old model car. Parts are worn out, and I can't get replacements for them. It's hard to get either of us started in the mornings. There was never a guarantee that we would keep on running. However, we're nearing the border. When we cross over, we will be given a warranty that lasts throughout eternity. This gift is for those who seek, knock, and find the Lord.

The joy of the Lord will be our spiritual strength for eternity.

THINK ABOUT IT

*Are you willing to take time to be still
so you can know God better?*

JOY

Rejoice in the Lord always: And again I say, Rejoice.
Philippians 4:4 KJV

Joy is a sparkle in our eyes that spills over into smiles and laughter. It is as refreshing as a cool drink of water on a hot summer day. When our souls are weary, joy is a cool breeze that blows away concerns.

A pleasant attitude can diminish our pain and despondency. Norman Cousins overcame a rare and painful autoimmune disease with large doses of vitamin C and laughter. Joy healed his physical and mental health. His immune system kicked in and destroyed his disease.

I find worship as a source of joy. Praise lifts my spirits when I express my love for what Jesus has done. Peace and gratitude fill my soul when I think of my many blessings.

What a comfort and joy it is to know God can bring something good from the worst of circumstances. When bad things happen, I try to think of what God can teach me in the experience. It may be patience and/or perseverance. It gives me some satisfaction to know I can learn something even in trials.

Something Good from a Bad Situation

I searched for a week, trying to find my keys. I looked everywhere I could think of. Finally, I gave up and bought a new post office key, which cost $100 here at the retirement center. It was frustrating to have to buy something I lost.

Less than 24 hours later I found my keys in a pants pocket. I had checked all those pockets three times. I had even taken all my slacks out of the closet and laid them on the bed to recheck them. My keys were in the corner of one of those pockets. The only thing that made me feel good was when I was looking for my keys, I cleaned my closet. I smiled when I thought of one good thing that came from my carelessness.

Even when I lose a loved one, I think of the joy they brought me when they were here. I focus on aspects of gratitude rather than spending so much time grieving my loss.

THINK ABOUT IT

Do you focus on positive or negative things in life?

The Fall Season

Like autumn leaves we fade, wither, and fall.
Isaiah 64:6 TLB

When cool weather blows in, it's time to get out our sweaters and jackets. Thankfully, we have homes today that keep us cozy. When I was a child, we only had an iron potbellied wood stove in the front bedroom and a cook-stove in the kitchen for heat. My sister, Ruth, screeched when I put my cold feet on her legs at night.

It was a treat when Momma heated bricks on the cook stove, wrapped them in a towel, and gave them to us to put in bed to warm our feet. Years later, we got natural gas and individual stoves throughout the house as well as a gas cookstove. Later, my folks got central heating.

Nature lets us know it's fall when leaves on the trees wrinkle, lose their green color, and drop to the ground like giant snowflakes. They snuggle close to what is left of warmth in the soil.

As we grow older, poor circulation causes our skin to wrinkle. But unlike leaves, we must be careful *not* to fall to the ground! It's time for us to take a deep breath as we prepare for a long winter's nap. The years are skedaddling by. Naps during the day may be the prelude for the time when we will close our eyes for the last time.

Unique Ways Animals Prepare for Winter

God prepares animals for the fall and winter in various ways. Some grow heavier and warmer coats. Others have hair that is hollow. These hairs have millions of little dead air spaces creating a type of insulation. Remarkably, the inner structure of the hollow hair changes between seasons, keeping the animal warmer in winter and cooler in summer, so they maintain a tolerable temperature.

Bears eat ferociously in the fall before they hibernate four months or more without eating or drinking. Some birds migrate long distances. For instance, the tiny hummingbird may migrate as far as 3,400 miles.

God, in His wisdom, created nature, mankind, and animals in various ways so they would survive throughout the various seasons. Animals hibernate, migrate, or their bodies adapt to keep them from freezing in winter or dying from heat in the summer. Our heavenly Father, in His creativity, designed His creatures in unique ways.

As humans, it is our choice to prepare for the fall and winter seasons of life when we must slow down and accept the changes in our bodies.

THINK ABOUT IT

Do you thank God for the ways He prepares us for the fall and winter seasons of our lives?

Blessed in Receiving

He has shown kindness by giving you rain from heaven and crops in their seasons; He provides you with plenty of food and fills our hearts with joy.
Acts 14:17 NIV

Over the years, the Lord has blessed me by taking care of me in incredible ways. I would have struggled financially in my later years, if I'd not convinced Carey we needed to buy a farm years before he died. Selling it after his death has helped provide for me in my declining years. God made sure my four trips to teach in the underground Bible school in China were paid for. He returned my money a hundred-fold when I gave money away.

One day, I was explaining to a group how the Lord had taken care of me. An unbeliever asked, "Why would you thank Him for things that were just a coincidence?"

"A few times may have been a coincidence," I said, "but I need to make up for the hundreds of times I've not thanked Him for what He *has* done. I've taken so much for granted and accepted many things as 'just happening.' I need to give Him credit for how He has provided for me all my life."

An Opportunity to Bless Someone in a Small Way

One hot Sunday at church, I asked our Bible class teacher how they were handling the heat. She shrugged her shoulders. "We're doing okay, although we don't have an air conditioner. When I'm outside working in the garden, I spray myself with water to cool off. Hopefully, we can buy an air conditioner next year."

Wow! Even though I knew the couple was poor, I couldn't believe they didn't have an air conditioner. We live in southwest Texas with high temperatures and humidity. The woman's husband has muscular dystrophy and is in a wheelchair. She has to care for him and can't work. I was determined to get an air conditioner for them.

THINK ABOUT IT

Do you thank God for the many things He has given you?

An Opportunity to Bless Others

We must help the weak, remembering the words the Lord Jesus himself said: "It is more blessed to give than to receive."
Acts 20:35 NIV

After learning a couple needed an air conditioner, I went to Lowes the next day and asked to speak to the manager. I wanted to see if he would give me a discount on an air conditioner for this needy family. The manager wasn't there that day, so the assistant manager came to talk to me. He asked what I wanted. I explained the family's plight. He said, "I'm not able to make that decision, but you *will* have to have a letter from the church to verify their situation."

I went to church, got the letter, and took it back the next morning. The assistant manager told me his manager wouldn't come until after lunch, but he would take the letter and give it to him. He assured me his boss would call me that afternoon with his decision. I waited for the call but didn't hear from him. I decided to go back to the store the following morning.

Persistence

Thank goodness, the manager was there. I asked if he read the letter. He said, "What letter? I've not seen one." By God's grace, I had a copy in the car. I ran out and got the letter for him. After reading it, he suggested we go back and look at the air conditioners. "Which one do you want?" I pointed to the one I'd picked, and he loaded it onto a cart.

Hesitantly, I asked, "How much is it going to cost me?"

"Not a dime. We set aside money the first of every month to give to charity. Today is the first, so we can cover the full amount." I was thrilled inside and out, as I had no idea I would get the air conditioner free.

I was choked up, and it was difficult to talk, but I asked him, "Can I give *you* something?" He looked puzzled but questioned, "What's that?"

I smiled. "I'd like to give you a hug." He grinned, stretched out his arms, and gave me a bear hug.

I took the air conditioner to church the next Sunday. Tears of gratitude trickled down the woman's cheeks when I told her about the gift the church was giving them. Thank You, Lord.

THINK ABOUT IT

How have you blessed someone's life by something you have given them or done for them?

Time to Move On

The righteous shall move onward and forward.
Job 17:9 TLB

I decided it was time for me to downsize and be closer to someone who could look after me. My youngest son, Chip, suggested I build a little house beside theirs. A friend would move her mobile home next door to help me if I needed her.

An architect designed the home, and I found a builder. It was time to prepare for this new season of life.

A niece visited shortly before the builder began construction. She said she didn't think this was wise since I was ninety-one and had fallen a few times. My children and I talked it over and agreed. We realized it wasn't a good idea for me to live alone any longer.

My son took me to visit retirement places. We went to one that served meals, cleaned the apartment once a week, changed my bedclothes and had a driver who could take me anywhere in town I needed to go. I would wear a call button if I fell or needed help. An assisted living area was attached if the time came when I was unable to care for myself. Everything I needed was there. The Lord seemed to whisper, "This is your new assignment."

Think About It

Has there ever been a time when you believe the Lord directed you where you were to go?

I Like to Teach, and I Like to Speak

We have different gifts according to the grace given to each of us… if it is teaching, then teach.
Romans 12:6-7 NIV

When I was getting settled in the retirement facility, I told the director that I liked to teach and I liked to speak. She said, "After you have been here a few months, we might use you some way."

New Doors Open

The first week after I moved, I attended a Bible class. I found the regular teacher had fallen and hurt her neck and moved to her daughter's home. A visiting teacher was scheduled to come that day, but she didn't show up. Rather than all of us going back to our apartments, I suggested we study Psalm 91. They agreed, and I taught the class.

After the Bible study, the woman who was supposed to begin teaching the Bible class went to the director and told her, "I think Louise is supposed to teach." It was only the second week after I moved when I was assigned to teach four classes a month. A week later, the director of the assisted living area asked if I would teach Bible classes in her area. I was happy to do so.

The activities director had seen one of my books and asked if I would write a devotional each week to print for the residents. I was pleased she asked me. A few months later, I volunteered to work with hospice. This *was* my new assignment.

THINK ABOUT IT

Have you ever felt the Lord lead you in a certain way to do His will?

My Bucket List

But in keeping with his promise we are looking forward to a new heaven and a new earth, where righteousness dwells.
2 Peter 3:13 NIV

Typically, the term "bucket list" refers to a place someone wants to go or something they want to do before they "kick the bucket." However, the place on my bucket list is where I long to go *after* I kick the bucket. Bottom line, I want more than anything else to go to heaven—not just for a visit or vacation, but to live throughout the ages.

You won't find heaven listed with any travel agent, but my desire to go there comes from reading God's Word and from those who have had an experience of life after death. There are those who believe they have had a glimpse of heaven. They say it is more than one could imagine. Colors, tones, emotions, and peace are far beyond reality.

The Excitement of Imagining What Heaven is Like

The thought of such a wondrous place brings tears to my eyes. These are tears of wonder and amazement. How marvelous to think of standing in the presence of the King of the Universe—for Him to reach out to draw me close to His bosom and say, "You're home, My child."

It is reported that the streets there are gold and clear as glass. The Tree of Life has leaves for the healing of nations. No more wars! All tears of sorrow and pain will be wiped away by the tender touch of the Master's hand. We will be comforted by the Holy Spirit and saturated to the bone with the Father's love.

Think About It

Do you ever sit and think what it would be like to live forever in the presence of God, prophets, apostles, and world-known evangelists?

LOOKING FORWARD TO HEAVEN

The twelve gates were twelve pearls each gate made of a single pearl. The great street of the city was of gold, as pure as transparent glass.
Revelation 21:21 NIV

Those of us who follow God and obey His commandments anxiously await the time when we will walk through those gates of pearl onto streets of gold. We are to be God's magnum opus—His work of art that has been transformed into His image.

Smiles and chuckles will replace all groaning and sorrow. A cool breeze of comfort and joy will brush across our cheeks rather than the storms of life we've experienced on planet earth. Calamities and disasters will be a thing of the past. We'll forget what it feels like to be sad. Total health and healing will bless us when all pain and disabilities are gone.

Perhaps we'll forget the struggles we faced here. We will be wrapped in a robe of righteousness woven with golden threads, with pockets of grace and mercy.

There will be neither regrets of the past nor fear of the future. Emotional and/or literal darkness will be dispelled by light. Those who've been close to Jesus will be solar powered reflecting His light. Praise will lift our spirits to highest heaven.

My imagination is great but is limited to a box far too small to include God's miraculous surprises.

The Holy Spirit, who has been our Comforter and Guide will live inside us, and Jesus will walk with us as our faithful Redeemer.

Think About It

Are you living in such a way God not only knows you, but claims you as His own child?

WHERE I'LL PROBABLY BE IN HEAVEN

Therefore I say unto you, take no thought for your life, what ye shall eat, or what ye shall drink; nor yet for your body, what ye shall put on. Is not the life more than meat, and the body than raiment?"
Matthew 6:25 KJV

I love to eat. I eat when I'm hungry, I eat when I'm stressed. I eat to celebrate, and I have a snack when I am bored.

It is interesting how many times the Bible speaks of eating together. It also tells us not to eat with sinners who refuse to repent. "What I meant was that you are not to keep company with anyone who claims to be a brother Christian but indulges in sexual sins, or is greedy, or is a swindler, or worships idols, or is a drunkard, or abusive. Don't even eat lunch with such a person" (1 Corinthians 5:11 TLB).

Immature Christians are Compared to Babies

"You are like babies who can drink only milk, not old enough for solid food. And when a person is still living on milk it shows he isn't very far along in the Christian life and doesn't know much about the difference between right and wrong. He is still a baby Christian!" (Hebrews 5:13 TLB).

When Scripture speaks of eating meat, it implies a person is a mature Christian. He not only tastes the Word but chews on it and digests it until it becomes a part of who he is.

I tell friends if I check out before they do, if they want to find me when they get to heaven, they'll probably find me at the Lord's banquet table where the desserts are served.

THINK ABOUT IT

Have you ever thought of God's Word being tasty?

Ways of Checking Out

I have fought the good fight, I have finished the race,
I have kept the faith.
2 Timothy 4:7 NIV

Leah's mother was in hospice. Leah was told if her siblings wanted to see their mother alive, they needed to come. She notified her two brothers and her sister, and they dropped everything so they could be with their mother.

They were all in their mother's room. She recognized them and could still talk. They told their mom how much they loved and appreciated her. Suddenly, she closed her eyes and began to speak as enthusiastically as she could muster. "There's Susan, Ray, and Robert." These were Christian loved ones who had died previously. Her children assumed she was seeing them in heaven. Their mom paused briefly and then asked. "But what is George doing there?" Her sons and daughters hadn't told their mom that her son, George, had died of a massive heart attack the week before. Chills ran up their spines as they realized she was looking across the River of Life and saw loved ones who'd gone on before. No doubt she was looking forward to a great reunion.

When Others were Dying

My sister called one evening to tell me our dad was failing fast. I left Dallas the following morning for the three-hour trip and drove straight to the hospital in Brownwood to see him. When I was about to leave, Daddy said, "Sweetheart, there is someone at the door, let them in." I looked, but there was no one there.

I left the hospital and drove to my sister's house. She lived a few minutes from the hospital. I had just walked in the door when the phone rang. My sister, Sis, answered it. It was the hospital. They told her, "Your father just passed away."

When Daddy told me there was someone at the door, did he see angels coming to get him?

When my husband, Carey, was dying, several doctors and interns came to his room, because they couldn't understand why he was in no pain.

Carey encouraged them. "Take the love of God all over this hospital." They stood there, not knowing how to respond. But one of the interns spoke up. "You're on the top floor, perhaps your love will flow down from this room."

THINK ABOUT IT

We wonder what it will be like when it comes time for us to cross over to the other side, but the Lord assures us there is no need for us to be fearful.

ALSO BY LOUISE L LOONEY

Splashes of Living Water
Marvels and Mysteries
Over the Hill Onto the Mountaintop
Make the Rest of Your Days the Best of Your Days
Out of Darkness into His Marvelous Light
Deep Roots
Newfound Hope
An Overcoming Walk of Peaks and Valleys

CONNECT WITH LOUISE

www.louisellooney.com
www.facebook.com/louiselooney

About the Author

Louise L Looney is an award-winning author who was given the Selah award for writing the best book on Christian living at the Blue Ridge Christian Writer's Conference. She was also named the Writer of the Year at the Colorado Christian Writer's Conference.

Louise has worn many hats other than being a wife, mother and writer.

- She taught in all levels of school including college, in the prison system, and worked as an Educational Diagnostician.
- She served as a Spiritual Director in a psychiatric hospital.
- For fifteen years, she managed Hidden Manna, a Christian retreat center.
- As a missionary, she went to China four times to teach in an underground Bible school of pastors, teachers and missionaries. They came from all over China to study the Bible for six hours a day for three months.
- Currently she teaches Bible Study lessons and prints out devotionals for residents at a retirement center.

Louise Looney
http://louisellooney.com
Blessings!

Made in the USA
Coppell, TX
13 February 2026

71997655R00094